CONTENTS

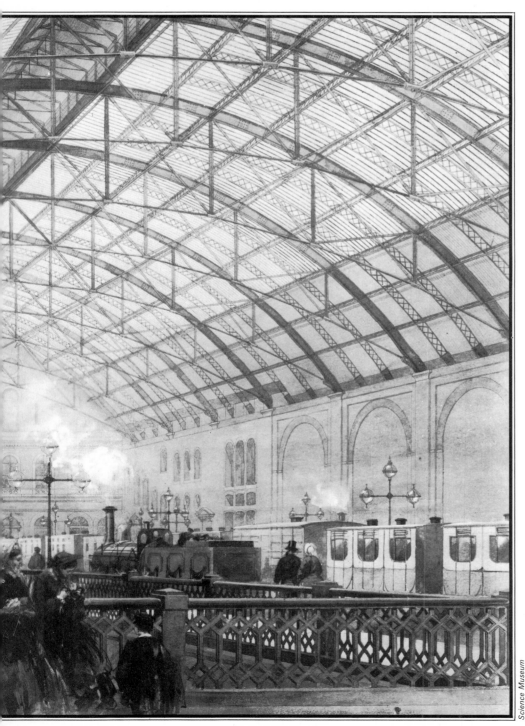

Science Museum

Peter Kalla-Bishop is a technical journalist. He began his career in 1935 as a railway engineer with the Southern Railway in England, and worked for seven years on military railways in Africa, Italy and Austria. He is the author of a number of railway histories, including *Italian Railways* and *Hungarian Railways*, and is a regular contributor to several publications, including *Railway Gazette International*, *Railway Magazine* and *Modern Railway*.

John Wood was an aircraft designer for a major British aircraft company for 20 years. Today, he and his team of artists have built up a considerable reputation in the field of technical illustration, and have produced more than 100 books, which have been sold in many countries, including the United States, France, Germany, Spain, Italy, Sweden and Japan. The specially commissioned illustrations in this book pay particular attention to the authentic colouring and detail of the locomotives of the period.

We are very greatful to A. D. Peters for kind permission to quote the passage from *Vile Bodies* by Evelyn Waugh on page 28.

Published 1977 by
The Hamlyn Publishing Group Limited
London New York Sydney Toronto
Astronaut House, Feltham, Middlesex, England

ISBN 0 600 38769 0

This edition © 1977 Phoebus Publishing
Company/BPC Publishing Limited
169 Wardour Street, London W1A 2JX

Part published in *First Trains*
© 1977 Phoebus Publishing Company/BPC
Publishing Limited

Made and printed in Great Britain by
Waterlow (Dunstable) Limited

ABOUT THIS BOOK

The Stockton & Darlington Railway opened in 1825 with George Stephenson at the controls of *Locomotion,* which he had designed. For the passengers this must have been quite a courageous journey; doctors had forecast high blood pressure and warned of the risk of tuberculosis in tunnels. Their fears proved groundless, the train unstoppable, and railway networks were established all over the world.

In France the Wagons-Lits company built coaches which were a byword in luxury; passengers could set off for the Russian wastes in the comfort of the *Orient Express.* The German States, divided politically, united to create a comprehensive railway system, while the Italian engineers battled with steep-sided valleys and tunnelled through mountain ranges. The vast American continent was linked coast to coast with railroads, which alarmed the buffalo but opened up the country to settlers and trade.

In the First World War the railways were mobilized to take troops and munitions to and from the front, and finally the Armistice itself was signed in a railway carriage.

The contemporary prints, engravings, drawings and photographs with the specially commissioned drawings of locomotives, illustrate the history of the railways up to 1920, when the motorcar and the aeroplane began to eclipse the Golden Age of Railways.

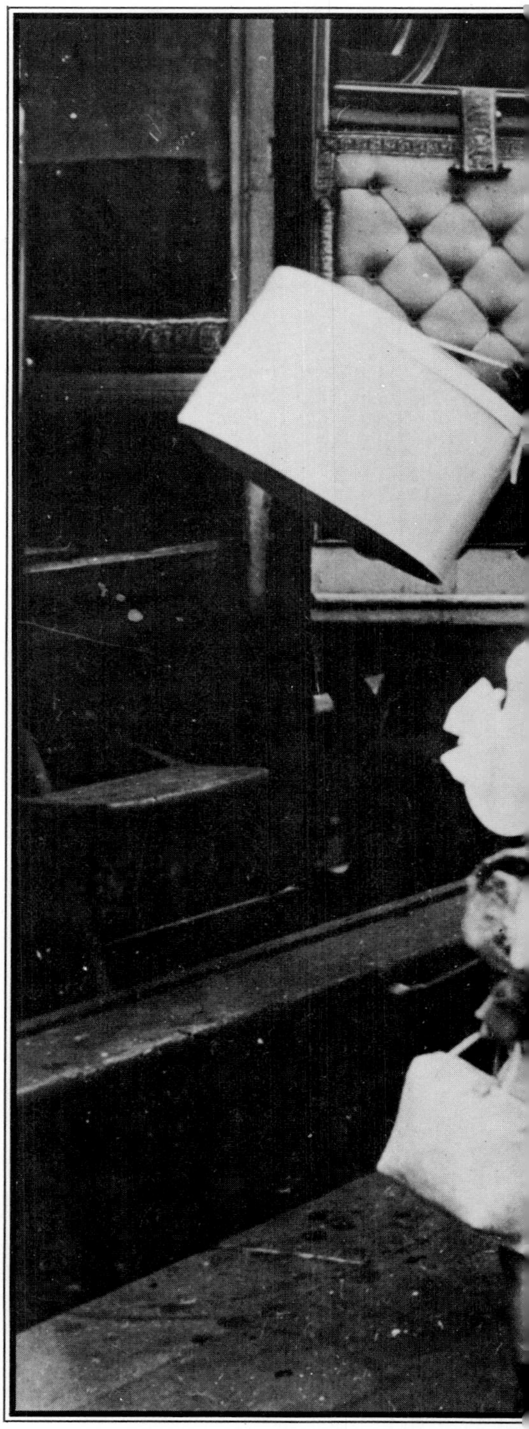

Consultant Editor: Peter Kalla-Bishop

Illustrated by: J. W. Wood and Associates

Written by: Harry Weaver

Editor: Robin Willcox

Art Editor: Sarah Reynolds

Designer: Frank Ainscough

Picture Research: Paul Snelgrove

Editorial Director: Graham Donaldson

THE
STOCKTON & DARLINGTON
RAILWAY COMPANY
Hereby give Notice,

THAT the FORMAL OPENING of their RAILWAY will take place on the 27th instant, as announced in the public Papers.—The Proprietors will assemble at the Permanent Steam Engine, situated below BRUSSELTON TOWER*, about nine Miles West of DARLINGTON, at 8 o'clock, and, after examining their extensive inclined Planes there, will start from the Foot of the BRUSSELTON descending Plane, at 9 o'clock, in the following Order :—

  1. THE COMPANY's LOCOMOTIVE ENGINE.
  2. The ENGINE's TENDER, with Water and Coals.
  3. Six WAGGONS, laden with Coals, Merchandize, &c.
  4. The COMMITTEE, and other PROPRIETORS, in the COACH belonging to the COMPANY.
  5. Six WAGGONS, with Seats reserved for STRANGERS.
  6. FOURTEEN WAGGONS, for the Conveyance of Workmen and others.

☞ The WHOLE of the above to proceed to STOCKTON.

  7. Six WAGGONS, laden with Coals, to leave the Procession at the DARLINGTON BRANCH.
  8. Six WAGGONS, drawn by Horses, for Workmen and others.
  9. Ditto   Ditto.
  10. Ditto   Ditto.
  11. Ditto   Ditto.

The COMPANY's WORKMEN to leave the Procession at DARLINGTON, and dine at that Place at ONE o'clock; excepting those to whom Tickets are specially given for YARM, and for whom Conveyances will be provided, on their Arrival at STOCKTON.

TICKETS will be given to the Workmen who are to dine at DARLINGTON, specifying the Houses of Entertainment.

The PROPRIETORS, and such of the NOBILITY and GENTRY as may honour them with their Company, will DINE precisely at THREE o'clock, at the TOWN-HALL, STOCKTON.— Such of the Party as may incline to return to DARLINGTON that Evening, will find Conveyances in waiting for their Accommodation, to start from the COMPANY's WHARF there precisely at SEVEN o'clock.

The COMPANY take this Opportunity of enjoining on all their WORK-PEOPLE that Attention to Sobriety and Decorum which they have hitherto had the Pleasure of observing.

The COMMITTEE give this PUBLIC NOTICE, that all Persons who shall ride upon, or by the sides of, the RAILWAY, on Horseback, will incur the Penalties imposed by the Acts of Parliament passed relative to this RAILWAY.

* Any Individuals desirous of seeing the Train of Waggons descending the inclined Plane from ETHERLEY, and in Progress to BRUSSELTON, may have an Opportunity of so doing, by being on the RAILWAY at St. HELEN's AUCKLAND not later than Half-past Seven o'clock.

RAILWAY-OFFICE, Sept. 19th, 1825.

ATKINSON's Office, High-Row, Darlington.

BIRTH OF THE

The handbills had been distributed and the crowds had gathered to watch what some considered a miracle and others the work of the devil. The date was September 27, 1825, and the world's first public railway with steam traction, the Stockton & Darlington, was about to open in north-east England.

The engineer was George Stephenson, a 45-year-old former colliery mechanic who had been nearly out of his 'teens before mastering the skills of reading and writing. Steam engines fascinated him, and he had designed and built *Locomotion*, the engine that was to pull a company coach-load of distinguished guests, plus 32 wagons laden with coal, merchandise, workmen and 'strangers' on this historic journey.

Stephenson had decided to drive the locomotive himself, and the spectators, mostly convinced that this madcap affair could end only in disaster (and rather looking forward to it), watched in awe as he climbed aboard the iron monster. From *Locomotion* came a sigh, a hiss and a clank, the wheels began to turn – and the Railway Age was born.

The Stockton & Darlington was not the world's first railway in a modern sense. The emphasis at the time was on freight – coal which needed to be moved in massive quantities to fuel the Industrial Revolution and goods which had to be delivered to the market place more swiftly and more cheaply than was possible by either road or canal.

George Stephenson (top right) was the father of the railways. His locomotive, called 'Locomotion' (right) pulled the first train at the formal opening of the Stockton & Darlington Railway.

Handbills (above) announced the coming event, which was thronged with people (below), many of whom expected disaster. Stephenson himself drove 'Locomotion' on the great day, September 27, 1825. 'Locomotion' is now preserved in Darlington.

6

RAILWAY AGE

Hence, after that first historic trip, passengers travelled on the Stockton & Darlington in horse-drawn coaches, and locomotives — which, in any case, tended to break down regularly — were reserved for coal and merchandise. Nevertheless, the Stockton & Darlington represented a significant step forward in the sense that it dragged the locomotive out of its birthplace, the colliery, and into the world.

Railway ride

The first crude steam locomotives to run on rails had actually been designed by Richard Trevithick nearly a quarter of a century earlier. In 1804, along an industrial private tramway, one of his locomotives pulled 10 tons of bar iron nine miles from ironworks near Merthyr Tydfil in Wales to the Glamorgan canal. Seventy sightseers, 'drawn thither by invincible curiosity', were also taken along for the ride.

The incident passed virtually unnoticed at the time, but Trevithick was the first man to marry steam power to rails, a marriage that was to last more than 150 years.

The first true modern railway was the Liverpool & Manchester, which opened on September 15, 1830. The route involved the construction of 63 bridges, one nine-arch viaduct 60ft high and a 60ft-deep cutting. For this line, Stephenson's son, Robert, designed his famous locomotive, the *Rocket*,

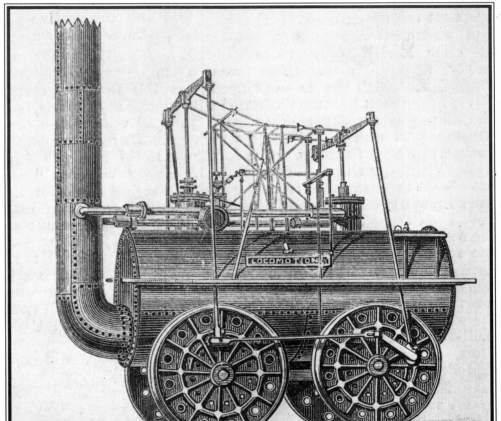

In 1808 Robert Trevithick's engine was tested near Euston Station in London (left), and earned the nickname 'Catch-me-who-can'; but the first true passenger carrying railway was the Liverpool & Manchester (below), which was opened on September 15, 1830, amid scenes of excitement and terror. During one of the necessary stops for water, an important guest, William Huskisson MP (right) stepped onto the track and was killed; this gave the railway's opponents excellent support. George Stephenson's son, Robert (centre right), designed the most famous locomotive for this line, the 'Rocket' (top right), shown here at the Rainhill Bridge Trials. It reached the astonishing speed of 30mph, thought to be 'dangerous'!

the first with a multi-tubular boiler combined with a cylinder-exhaust blastpipe directed up the chimney to draw the fire.

Of the *Rocket*, which achieved, for the first time, speeds of more than 30mph in trials, one eye-witness wrote: "It seemed indeed to fly, presenting one of the most sublime spectacles of mechanical ingenuity and human daring the world ever beheld."

On that first day, amid scenes of great enthusiasm, eight trains left Liverpool for Manchester. Among the honoured guests — although an opponent of railways on the grounds that they "would encourage the lower orders to move about" — was the Duke of Wellington. He travelled in a state carriage whose workmanship was "perfect and tasteful; superb Grecian scrolls and balustrades, richly gilt, supported a massy handrail running round the carriage . . . The drapery was of rich crimson cloth, and the whole was surmounted by the ducal coronet . . ."

First casualty

Another guest was William Huskisson, economist and MP for Liverpool. When the train stopped in the course of the journey to take on water, he got down on the track and was knocked down and killed by a locomotive travelling in the opposite direction, an event since claimed as the world's first railway accident. This was all that the influential weekly *John Bull,* an implacable enemy of this new form of transport, needed to launch into a fresh tirade:

". . . all their lives (were) at the mercy of a tin pipe or a copper boiler, or the accidental dropping of a pebble on the line of way. We denounce the mania as destructive of the country in a thousand particulars — the whole face of the kingdom is to be tattooed with these deformities. — huge mounds are to intersect our beautiful valleys; the noise and stench of locomotive steam engines are to disturb the quietude of the peasant, the farmer and the gentleman . . ."

John Bull was by no means alone in its opposition. Like the canals and turnpike roads before them, railways had to have powers for the compulsory purchase of land and these powers could be granted only by an Act of Parliament. The proceedings, similar to a modern planning inquiry, were normally long drawn-out and costly, with every conceivable objection raised and expert witnesses produced to back up the objectors, just as they are today.

The fact that man now had a means of transport able to carry him faster than could the muscles of a horse made the 'dangerous speed' of trains one obvious and recurrent target of attack. In the course of obtaining

the Liverpool & Manchester Act, which needed two attempts before he was successful, George Stephenson was asked: "What if a locomotive travelling at 12mph runs into a cow? Would it be fatal (to the train)?"

"It would be worse for the cow," he replied.

Landlords protested that locomotives hurtling through the countryside would dry up their cows, set fire to their hayricks, frighten away foxes and ruin the hunt. Farriers, blacksmiths, harness-makers, horse breeders and dealers, carriage-makers and the keepers of roadside inns complained that their livelihood would be ruined.

Health hazard

Doctors stepped forward to assert that travelling through railway tunnels would produce chills, colds, catarrh and consumption; that a gradient of 1:60 would be bad for gout sufferers; that passengers with high blood pressure would run the risk of apoplexy if they travelled in fast trains.

Even as late as the 1880s, Dr J. Russell Reynolds, consultant physician at University College Hospital in London, offered the opinion that passengers who appeared to doze off in trains were not actually asleep but were in a kind of stupor induced by 'concussion of the brain.'

Some of the most determined opponents of railways were the seats of learning. Eton College, for example, had a clause inserted into the Great Western Act stipulating that the company could not even build a station in the neighbouring town of Slough, let alone in Eton itself. Once the line was in operation, the Great Western evaded the clause by stopping its trains without building a platform and by selling tickets in a nearby public house.

Eton College was furious and tried to obtain a court injunction, but the action was dismissed with costs, which was probably just as well as, only a month later, the college found itself applying for a special train to take pupils to Queen Victoria's coronation.

In this climate, building a railway was a daunting and expensive undertaking. Initially, surveyors, who had no right to enter private property, frequently found themselves set upon by fierce bulls and armed gamekeepers, urged on by landowners who still believed that an Englishman's home, and the acres around it, were his castle.

Then there was the Act, which cost money and time. The London & Birmingham Railway, completed in 1838, spent £72 000 — say £1 million in present day terms — before obtaining its Act, and the famous engineer Isambard Kingdom Brunel, builder of the Great Western, once underwent a cross-examination lasting 11 days.

But the objectors could only delay, not halt, a process which the country needed and the forward-looking minority of people demanded. The Liverpool & Manchester proved an instant success and, contrary to the expectations of the builders, the bulk of its revenue came from passengers rather than freight.

The popularity of the L. & M. sparked off the railway fever which swept the country and, in little more than a decade, Britain had most of the elements of a modern railway system. These included railway stations with waiting and refreshment rooms, a booking office and raised platforms; level crossing gates; ticket collectors; water towers; the modern rail shape mounted on timber sleepers; separate tracks for up and down lines; a signalling system; loading gauges; carriages with compartments. There were also 'steam trumpets' for locomotives (invented after a collision with a horse-drawn cart on a level crossing of the Leicester & Swannington Railway in 1833), and even the first railway hotel, opened at the Euston terminus of the London & Birmingham in 1839, soon to be followed by others at the main railway termini.

Britain also possessed what was, in all essentials, a modern steam locomotive. Robert Stephenson's *Rocket* was swiftly followed by the *Patentee*, which appeared in 1833. By 1840 the *Patentee*-type was the standard steam locomotive of its day, built not only by Robert Stephenson & Co., but by other British and foreign manufacturers under licence, and it was to prove one of the most

durable designs of all time. The Belgian State Railway had improved versions built until after 1890 and some near-relations are still at work in India, South Africa and other countries today.

At the end of the decade, Britain had 1497 miles of railway compared with 97 in 1830. They included the first trunk line, Liverpool-Manchester-Crewe-Birmingham, which opened throughout in 1837, London-Birmingham (1838), Derby-Nottingham-Leicester-Rugby (1839–40) London-Romford (1839) and London-Southampton (1840). They were followed swiftly by London-Brighton (1840–41), London-Bristol (1841) and London-Dover (1842–44).

In Scotland, the first public steam railway was the Garnkirk & Glasgow opened in 1831. It was followed by the Glasgow-Paisley-Kilmarnock-Ayr line (1840) and the Glasgow-Edinburgh (1842). In Ireland, the Dublin-Kingstown (Dun Laoghaire) route opened in 1834, followed by the Ulster Railway, from Belfast to Lisburn, in 1839 and the Dublin-Drogheda line in 1844.

Blood, sweat and muscle

The railways, a concept on the same scale as the pyramids and the great medieval cathedrals, were built largely by blood, sweat and muscle, with the aid of a certain amount of gunpowder. The men who wielded the picks and shovels were called 'navvies' from the navigators who had built the canals of an earlier century.

As Terry Coleman says in his book *The*

Railway Navvies: "They wore moleskin trousers, double-canvas shirts, velveteen square-tailed coats, hobnail boots, gaudy handkerchiefs, and white felt hats with the brims turned up. They would pay 15 shillings, a great price (note: nearly a week's wages), for a sealskin cap, and their distinct badge was the rainbow waistcoat. They were often known to the contractor, and to everyone else, only by their nicknames — Gipsy Joe, Bellerophon, Fisherman, Fighting Jack.

"The railways came suddenly. After the surveyors, the navvies; perhaps, as at Blisworth in the late thirties, 3000 of them on a five-mile stretch of line. They lodged when they could in the villages, and, when there were no villages, they herded into turf shanties thrown up by the men themselves, or by the contractors. A few brought their wives. Others lived, nineteen to a hut, with one shared woman. They were paid once a month — sometimes not so frequently — and usually in a public house, and then for days after they drank their pay, sold their shovels for beer, rioted, and went on a randy."

Clergymen railed against them, genteel Victorian ladies tried to save them. However, in addition to drinking, eating, cursing, fighting, fornicating and other excesses, the navvy was addicted to hard work and proud of his strength. By the end of the century, navvies had laid 20 000 miles of railways in Britain, plus a few thousand more in the rest of the world, and had given the simile, 'to work like a navvy', a firm place in the English language.

Locomotive No. 15 of the Caledonian Railway (below) was developed by A. Allan and J. Buddicom in the 1840s. It is of the Crewe type, which was characterized by having both inside and outside frames; the cylinders and slide bars were mounted between the two frames. Originally built for the British railways, it was adopted by several railways abroad. Buddicom was **later made locomotive engineer on the Paris & Rouen Railway, and the engine was then also built in France. Above right: Platelayers at work on Saltash station; Brunel's bridge over the Tamar estuary is in the background. Tracklaying machinery introduced within the last 30 years has replaced the armies of men which were required in the early days of railways.**

Mansell

National Portrait Gallery

LEA

The railways employed the best engineers and the best brains. Nowadays few people give much thought to their early achievements – Brunel's enormous tunnel at Box, near Bath . . . Locke's great cuttings through the South Downs between Basingstoke and Winchester . . . the viaduct, 90 feet high, which still dominates the Stockport skyline. But, in their time, they were as great a marvel as the supersonic aircraft and the rockets which were to take men to the Moon a century later.

Primitive conditions

Although passengers flocked to make use of the railways, early travelling conditions were primitive. First-class carriages were initially modelled on horse-drawn coaches. The only form of lighting at night was a smelly oil lamp in the roof; there was no form of heating; and there was no means of communicating with either the neighbouring compartment or the guard.

Second-class carriages had roofs, but were not enclosed at the sides, and the early third-class passengers travelled in what were to all intents and purposes open wagons. Packed as many as 60 to a truck, they were buffeted by the wind, deluged with rain, hail, snow and soot, and frequently had their clothes set alight by cinders from the locomotive or sparks from the carriage wheels, the trucks having holes in the floorboards to let out the rainwater.

Something was done to improve the lot of the traveller with two general Railway Acts, passed by Parliament in 1842 and 1844, which can be claimed as the first modern land transport legislation in the world. Every country now has some sort of transport law, which has been extended to cover roads and the skies as this became necessary, but they all stem from the original British legislation.

Responsibility for piloting the Acts through Parliament fell upon a rising young politician named William Ewart Gladstone. The first was concerned with railway safety. It provided for the appointment of an Inspector of Railways – an officer of the Royal Engineers was the first to hold the post – starting a tradition which has persisted to this day. His duties included approving all railway arrangements as well as laying down the basic rules that have to be obeyed by every railwayman to ensure safety.

In modern times this has led to a practice which Gladstone can hardly have foreseen: railway unions have seized upon working to rule as a means of disrupting and slowing down services when they find themselves involved in an industrial dispute.

Gladstone's second Railway Act dealt with planning and conditions of travel. It was laid down that each railway bill, and the objections to it, should be considered by a select committee of the House of Commons, made up of members whose constituencies were not affected by the proposed railway, and that one of the committee's duties would be to ensure that there was no duplication of railway routes.

This second stipulation had two effects. It ensured the best use of the limited investment capital available in the country at that time, and it encouraged entrepreneurs to undertake railway routes which, although desirable from a national standpoint, did not appear to offer a very large profit. But, although the profit might be small, lack of competition made what profit there was as certain as such things can be.

Gladstone's 1844 legislation also laid down the duty of each railway to run, on every line daily, a train to which third-class passengers were admitted and which served each station on the line; stipulated that third-class passengers in these trains had to be accommodated in 'covered carriages'; and set a national fare of a penny a mile. This was the beginning of the fixing of transport fares by political means, a practice that continues to give trouble today.

Gladstone did nothing, however, about two of the commonest causes of distress to early railway travellers – lack of food and lack of facilities for answering the calls of nature. Trains commonly halted 10 or 20 minutes at principal stations to make good these failings. Complaints about the quality of railway food – pork pies were one of the commonest targets – go back to the earliest days. Swindon, where the Great Western had given the catering contract to a hotel owner, was a notorious blackspot. Even Brunel, who had built the line, found that his influence was of no avail. "I have long ceased to make complaints at Swindon," he wrote in a letter. "I avoid taking anything there if I can help it."

In contrast, the six-course meal provided at Normanton in Yorkshire was highly praised, and, at Wolverton on the London & Birmingham, a woman supervisor aided by 'seven very young ladies' not only refreshed the weary traveller with wholesome pork pies (made on the premises), buns, cakes and sundry drinks, but is credited also with having given Europe the concept of the bar, the barmaid and counter service.

The first lavatory on a British train was one which the Great Western provided for Queen Victoria in 1850. It was no more sophisticated than the arrangement in most bedrooms throughout the land. Not even first-class travellers could hope for a convenience, unless they provided their own, until the 1870s when some early London & North Western sleeping cars were equipped with closets. The lavatories in these first railway toilets were fashionably decorated with flowers.

The stopping of a train at a station inevitably saw a stampede of passengers seeking relief, and, if the file looked formidably long, lady's maids, being lesser creatures, were often expected to make do with a discreetly-placed coal scuttle. On branch lines, beleaguered passengers would hop down when the train stopped at a signal and seek the sanctuary of a wayside copse or hedge, an uncertain procedure which could mean waiting for the next train.

Gauging it right

In the mid-1840s, the government stepped in again to resolve another railway matter – the question of gauge, the distance between the inside faces of the rails.

George Stephenson took as his track gauge the one that he found in general use for colliery tramroads in the north of England, 1435mm (4ft 8½in), now known as standard gauge. No one knows how this gauge was first hit upon, but it is supposed to be the result of fitting flanges to the wheels of horse-drawn road vehicles and thus to be related to the customary distance between cart wheels.

Most railways in Europe, and all in North America, are standard gauge today, together with a large number elsewhere, including the railway system of China. The early days of railways, however, saw a proliferation of gauges, particularly in the United States and

Conditions on early railways were quite primitive, with an oil lamp but no heating for first-class passengers and more or less open wagons in third class. Gladstone (far left) championed the early Railway Acts which established safety conditions and ensured that every line ran a train at least once a day with covered carriages for third-class passengers. However, there were no buffet cars, and trains might stop for ten minutes at main stations, where a hectic snack could be bolted down (left).

The gauges laid down differed, though the most common was based on the width between horse-carriage wheels – 4ft 8½in, and this was adopted as standard in 1846. Isambard Kingdom Brunel (right) used the widest gauge for the Great Western – 7ft 0¼in but they were converted to standard by 1892.
Conditions for the crews were even more Spartan than for third-class passengers; the locomotive No. 15 on the Caledonian Railway (below) as it was in 1847, had no protective cab.

Mansell

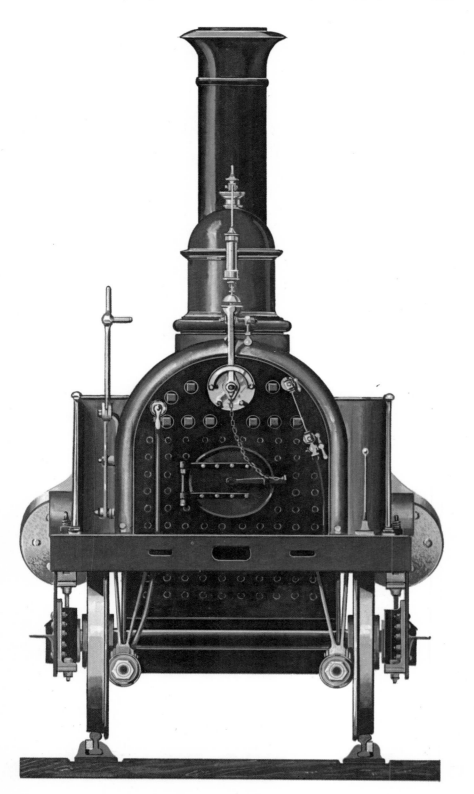

the British Empire, with consequent difficulty when tracks linked up within or between countries, passengers having to transfer from one train to another and freight having to be unloaded and loaded again – a very costly operation.

The majority of early British railways were standard gauge as nearly all were built by, or under the influence of, the prestigious George Stephenson. There were various arguments put forward nevertheless in favour of broader gauges – that they gave greater stability to rolling stock, provided a smoother ride, lessened the likelihood of carriages overturning in a derailment and gave more space between the wheels to install the working parts of locomotives.

Brunel, convinced of the advantages of a broader gauge, already in use in the United States and Russia, chose the widest of all, 7ft 0¼in, for the Great Western route which, starting at Paddington in 1838, eventually reached Penzance in Cornwall and Milford Haven in South Wales. The confusion and complaints which resulted when the Great Western met standard gauge at Gloucester in 1844 led first to a Royal Commission, then to the Railway Gauge Act of 1846.

The legislation laid down that, apart from the Great Western, all railways in England, Scotland and Wales should be standard gauge. The Great Western later found it expedient to convert line by line until the last of the 7ft 0¼in gauge disappeared in 1892.

Ireland had three gauges at first, standard (Dublin-Kingstown), 6ft 2in (the Ulster Railway) and 5ft 2in (Dublin-Drogheda). An Act of 1845 laid down that the standard gauge for all Ireland should be 5ft 3in, a decision which may be considered fair as it meant that everybody had to change, although it was, in fact, a sop to metrication enthusiasts in Parliament as it works out at 1600mm exactly.

Speculation and swindles

By this time anyone with money to invest was gripped by railway mania. Shares in companies with projected routes, which had not yet been surveyed and would never be built, were sold and re-sold. In one month of 1845, according to the *Manchester Guardian*, 357 railways-to-be had been advertised with a total capital of £332 million.

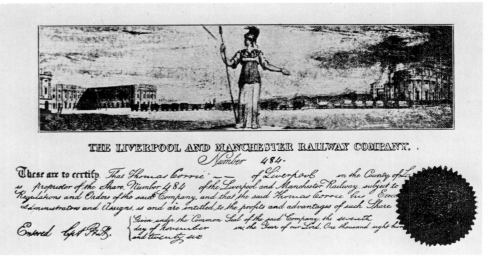

Into this arena of frenzied finance stepped George Hudson, a rich Yorkshire linen draper, who earned the Stock Exchange title of 'The Railway King'. He was also one of the first millionaire swindlers. By the start of 1849 he was one of the richest men in the country; by the end of the year, having been caught out in shady share transactions, he was a bankrupt and thousands more were ruined in the collapse of the railway share market.

But, although he had been caught with his finger in the jam, Hudson left behind some solid achievements. He had a considerable influence on some of the early railway routes in the Midlands and North-east and also ensured that the North Eastern Railway was one of the largest in the country. In 1868, hearing of his poverty, a grateful Conservative Party in Sunderland bought him a substantial £600-a-year annuity.

In spite of the speculative schemes, the railways continued to expand. The first through railway from London to Scotland came in 1847–48 when the London & North Western Railway (as the old London & Birmingham had been renamed after complicated amalgamations in 1846 which took it as far as Carlisle) linked up with the freshly-opened Caledonian Railway route from Glasgow to Carlisle. On the east coast, the Glasgow-Edinburgh line was extended to Berwick-on-Tweed in 1846 and was connected to the English system when the Royal Border Bridge was finished in 1850.

Bridging the gaps

Robert Stephenson bridged the Tyne in 1849 and the Menai Straits in 1850, and, by the time King's Cross Station in London opened in 1852, the greater part of the British railway system was complete or in an advanced state of planning, with only a few important pieces — such as Brunel's bridge over the Tamar (1859), the Severn Tunnel (1886) and the Forth Bridge (1890) — needed to complete the engineering jigsaw puzzle.

In the mid-nineteenth century, the railway traveller — and men in particular — often had to cope with danger as well as discomfort. Trains were frequented by cardsharps, thimble-riggers, pickpockets, robbers and murderers, whose fondness for dressing up as clergymen often gave the impression that the

Before railway gauges were standardized passengers had to transfer lines. Stations such as Gloucester, where the 7ft 0¼in gauge met the standard, saw scenes of chaos (below) for many years. Railway shares boomed and bust like the South Sea Bubble Company. Speculators made fortunes, although George Hudson (far left), a millionaire swindler, nicknamed 'The Railway King', was finally bankrupted when the market crashed. Left: A share certificate for the Liverpool & Manchester Railway Co. To link the island of Anglesey with the mainland Robert Stephenson designed the 1834-ft long tubular Britannia Bridge, seen here (right) behind Thomas Telford's Menai Suspension Bridge.

Church of England had ordered a mass exchange of incumbents.

These threats to the wallet and the person could not be avoided by wisely choosing a compartment occupied by a lady. In the absence of corridors many of these apparent ladies turned out to be blackmailers who, unless their demands were met, proved only too ready to march up to a porter at the end of the journey and make accusations of 'improper advances'. The word around the clubs was that it was safer to travel in male company while bearing in mind the advice offered by *The Railway Travellers' Handy Book* of 1862: "In going through a tunnel it is always as well to have the hands and arms ready disposed for defence so that in the event of an attack the assailant may be immediately beaten back or restrained."

Murder on the move

The first victim of a murder on a British train was Thomas Briggs, a 69-year-old clerk, battered to death and thrown onto the line while travelling in London on the 21.50 from Broad Street to Poplar in July 1864. The motive appeared to be robbery as his gold watch and chain, and gold-rimmed eyeglass, were found to be missing.

Suspicion fell upon Franz Müller, an immigrant from Cologne, who was found to have boarded the sailing ship *Victoria* at London Docks, bound for the United States. Two police officers travelled (by rail, of course) to Liverpool, caught the steamship *City of Manchester*, waited 20 days in New York, and finally arrested Müller as he stepped ashore from his sailing ship.

The case led some railway companies to cut small circular observation holes, known as 'Müller's lights', to make it possible to see from one compartment into another, an innovation much criticized by Victorian courting couples.

Gradually, the railways became more sophisticated and by 1890 a journey by train was very often a relaxation rather than the endurance test it had been in the past. Foot-warmers, which were cans filled with hot water and replenished at stops every two hours or so, were supplemented by chemical heaters, relying on the reaction between acetate of soda and water. From the 1860s, gas lighting started to take over from smelly

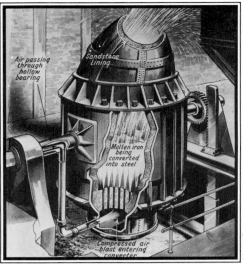

Mansell

Mansell

Railway tracks and wheels were made from wrought iron until Henry Bessemer (far left) invented in 1856 a method of making steel, which was cheaper and more reliable. Left: Cutaway drawing of Bessemer's converter. On short journeys it was an advantage to have a locomotive that could run in either direction, avoiding frequent turnings of the engine. The North Eastern Railway No. 947 (below), built in 1874, had not only this advantage, but carried all its own coal and water. Signalling developed from flag or lamp signals made by railway policemen (right) to the elaborate signal box at London Bridge Station (far right) in the 1850s. An American sense of luxury was introduced into Britain in 1865 by the Pullman Car (below right).

oil lamps, changed periodically by railway-men scampering agilely along carriage roofs when the train made a halt.

The springing of carriages improved, and bogies – an American development, although suggested by Robert Stephenson as a means of coping with the poor state of their tracks – began to replace four-wheel and six-wheel coaches. The under-privileged British third-class passenger found his status improved in 1872 when the Midland decided to carry third-class ticketholders on all its trains instead of excluding them from the best and fastest expresses.

Initially, the Midland's rivals saw this as the encroachment of a new political spectre, Socialism, but changed their minds when they saw the profits to be made out of third-class travel. The Midland went even further two years later, abolishing its second-class category altogether and introducing upholstered seats into all third-class carriages.

The Great Northern brought in sleeping cars in 1873, the London & North Western in 1874. Although rough and ready arrangements had existed to enable railway travellers to lie down and sleep since the 1830s,

night travel had been unpopular and avoided up to this time. In the United States, however, the vastly greater distances to be travelled led George Mortimer Pullman to convert a car of the Chicago & Alton Railroad into a sleeping car – ancestor of the Continental *couchette* – with a hinged upper berth which could be used to store bedding by day.

Luxury sleep

This innovation in 1859 was followed in 1865 by his first purpose-built sleeping Pullmans, which doubled as luxury coaches by day. In 1873, James Allport of the Midland Railway came to an agreement under which Pullman built coaches to American designs for the Midland at his own expense, received the supplementary fares that were payable, but had, in turn, to pay a fee to the company.

Pullman sleepers did not survive long, British companies deciding that they could do just as well with their own, but the Pullman coach endured as a symbol, and a fact, of luxury day travel by rail in Britain until well into the second half of the twentieth century.

The dining car was another transatlantic importation. The first restaurant car ran on

the Great Western Railway of Canada in 1867, the first in Britain 12 years later. This innovation put a gradual end to the long stops at major stations for rest and refreshment, and – to everyone's relief – led to the toilet becoming an integral part of railway carriage design.

Throughout the period there were various technical developments. Within a short time of Henry Bessemer developing his new steel-making process in 1856, cheap and reliable steel began to take over from wrought iron as the basic material of rails and wheels, and for many other railway needs. Locomotives became increasingly efficient, and modified fireboxes enabled them to burn coal instead of coke, a fuel which had been forced on the companies by Parliament's determination that, for environmental reasons, the early locomotives should not emit smoke.

Signalling, too, underwent constant modification from early times – red and green flags, red and green boards, coloured lights, followed by semaphore signals which made their initial appearance at New Cross in London in 1841. Along with the railway marched William Cooke's electric telegraph,

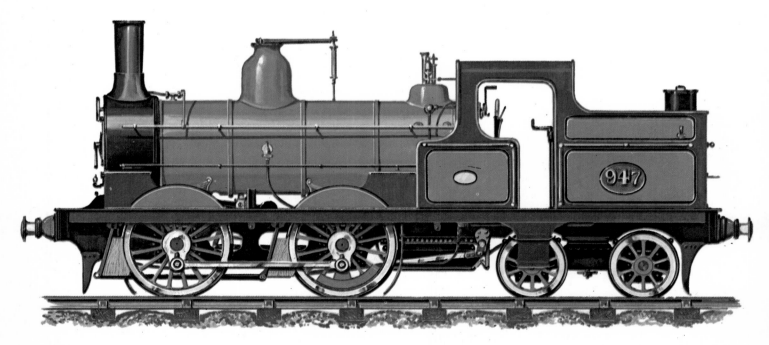

17

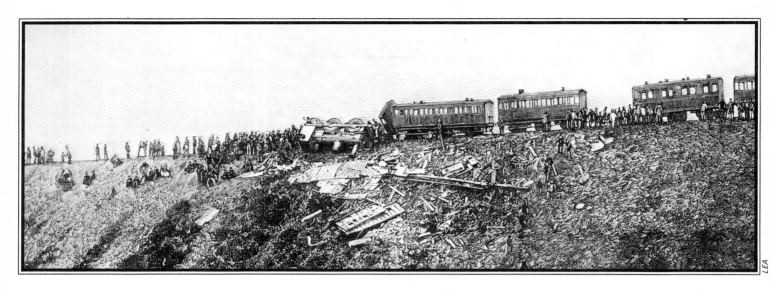

which was tried out for the first time on the London & Birmingham Railway in 1837 and installed between Paddington and West Drayton on the Great Western in 1839.

Block working – the system, made possible by the telegraph, which allowed only one train at a time into a section of track between signal boxes – was introduced on a series of sections of the Norfolk Railway between Norwich and Yarmouth in 1844. The first interlocking signal frame, designed to prevent a signalman from causing a collision through a mistake, was installed at a junction between London Bridge and New Cross two years later.

But the spread of the electric telegraph and other safety devices was slow in Britain, and railways remained accident-prone in the public view. The sad record of the London, Chatham & Dover, although no worse than some other lines, earned it the nickname of the 'London, Smash 'em & Turnover', and, as a circulation stunt, *Tit-Bits* magazine offered £100 free insurance to the next-of-kin of any passenger killed in a railway accident, providing he had a copy of the publication in his pocket.

Quakers were closely involved in the early development of British railways, particularly in the Midlands and north, and the original *Bradshaw*'s timetable was issued by a Friend, eager to help the traveller (until this century *Bradshaw* carried the Quaker inscription 'First Mo.' instead of 'January' and so on). The railway companies' inability to keep to their early schedules was demonstrated, however, by the fact that the newspaper known as *The Pink 'Un*, which ran a contest for the biggest lie, awarded first prize to the competitor who sent in a railway timetable.

It has been said that any fool can start a train, but that it takes a skilled man to stop it. This was particularly true until the 1860s, for the efforts of several men on hand brakes had to be coordinated. Then the vacuum brake and George Westinghouse's air brake, providing braking power over the entire train, were developed in the United States. Both were followed by fail-safe automatic versions, but the ability to use these properly is one of the engine-driver's remaining skills today.

Despite these developments, a train held

up in a tunnel at King's Cross was run into by the three following trains, one after the other, as late as 1881, and it was not until an accident near Armagh in 1889, when half an excursion train broke loose, ran backwards down a hill and collided with a train coming up behind it, that the automatic brake was made mandatory on all passenger trains in the British Isles. At the same time, block working was laid down as obligatory for all railways.

As for speeds, an average of rather more than 40mph over a complete journey was considered adequate – and, indeed, all that anyone could desire – until the late 1880s. In 1888, for instance, the trip of nearly 400 miles from London to Edinburgh took roughly 10 hours by either the east or west routes. That summer the companies concerned entered into a speed competition with the result that up to two and a half hours were knocked off the run. Eventually, a schedule of eight hours was agreed for the western route and 15 minutes less for the eastern route (subsequently increased to eight hours as well). These times were to remain unchanged until after the Second World War.

Travel for the masses

The social effects of the train were enormous. At the dawn of the Railway Age, travel was a slow and expensive luxury. The 175-mile journey from London to Exeter took 19 hours by stagecoach, including stops for meals. Hence, thousands of country folk had never seen the sea, thousands of town dwellers had never known the pleasure of strolling down a country lane with only the song of a skylark for company. For a country girl to go into service in a house more than a few miles from her home frequently meant exile from her family for life.

The railways changed all that. By 1846, for example, you could travel from London to Exeter in a mere six and a half hours by train and at a cost far cheaper than the stagecoach had been. As the Duke of Wellington had rightly feared, the 'lower orders' were quick to take advantage of the opportunity to 'move about' as the prosperity of the Industrial Revolution put more money into their pockets. Nevertheless, at least half the population could not afford this pleasure unless they took an excursion, which was an early railway offering. In 1840, benefitting

from the fact that third-class passengers had to stand in open wagons and were thus easier to pack in, the Midland Counties Railway carried no fewer than 2400 merrymakers on a single outing.

The possibilities were not lost on a young supporter of the temperance movement named Thomas Cook, who hired a train in 1841 and took 500 people from Leicester to Loughborough, 10 miles away, for a day out. The charge for this, his very first excursion, was a shilling, and the proceedings included a visit to a stately home, followed by a cricket match in the park.

From there it was but a stepping stone to Continental travel. A popular route had been London Bridge to Ostend, which began to lose favour once the South Eastern Railway reached the Channel port of Dover. Traffic with the Continent increased from there, both to Ostend and Calais, and bigger wooden paddle steamers were built, followed by bigger iron paddle steamers and finally twin-screw vessels. The London, Brighton & South Coast Railway opened the Newhaven-Dieppe route in 1862. Other sea links were Harwich-Rotterdam and Queenborough (on the Isle of Sheppey)-Flushing.

Thomas Cook sent thousands of better-heeled citizens to savour the pleasures of Continental capitals, Mediterranean sunshine and climbing in the Alps. The traffic was by no means one-way. At the time of the Great Exhibition in 1851, passengers were arriving at Dover at the rate of 2000 a week, most of them having made the crossing from Calais in 90 minutes.

The chief cause of complaint at Dover in those days was not the customs but the porters, who early gained a reputation as "a worthless set of good-for-nothing fellows," adept at fleecing innocent foreigners. "It is easier to wash an Ethiop white than make a Dover porter honest," said a writer in 1856.

Like the Industrial Revolution, the coming of the railways spelled an end to the old easy-going pastoral way of life. They needed men who were disciplined and responsible – ex-soldiers were in strong demand – and men who possessed the basic educational skills of reading and writing.

The railways also contributed to, and possibly even gave rise to, the concept of a managerial elite. In 1861, for instance, the

Safety on the railways was improved by the introduction of block working, which allowed only one train on the line between signals at a time. However, the Armagh accident in 1889 (left) showed that braking regulations were inadequate. The law was changed, making continuous automatic brakes mandatory, so that individual coaches were automatically braked to a standstill when detached from the locomotive. The locomotive below, on the South Eastern Railway, was built in 1879; the tubes to the smoke box are part of the automatic vacuum brake. With greater safety and comfort, passengers were tempted by such advertisements as the one distributed by Thomas Cook (below). The first-class continental tour lasted a month.

London, Chatham & Dover wooed James Staats Forbes from the post of general manager of the Dutch Rhenish Railway with an offer of a monumental salary and emoluments equivalent to £136 000 a year at today's rates. Taking into account the minimal rates of income tax levied at the time, this is probably the highest remuneration ever paid to a railway official.

Fresh fruit for the town dwellers . . . fresh saltwater fish for the countryman . . . cheap books and newspapers . . . closer liaison between MPs and their constituencies . . . annual seaside holidays — the railways reached out to touch all aspects of life. The resort of Blackpool on the north-east coast had grown so big by 1876 that it achieved the civic status of a borough, and the greater part of the coast of England and Wales, including some of the distant corners of Corn-

wall, were besieged in high summer by hordes of trippers and holidaymakers.

Not all the news was good. The railway bought up many fine canals and allowed them to rot; cheap bricks and slates, hauled by the thousand in railway goods trucks, largely destroyed local architecture using local materials, and scarred the country with rows of drab houses; and, although they remained peaceful until the coming of the motor car, roads were also neglected.

But, whether a miracle or the work of the devil, the coming of the 'iron horse' was a boon to Britain and the world, not merely in the practical sense that it opened up the market places and turned goods which had once been luxuries into common comforts that everyone could afford. The railway also broadened the horizons of every man, woman and child with the price of a seat.

19

RAILWAY RIVALRY IN BRITAIN

The year 1890 saw the world poised on the brink of what has been rightly called 'The Golden Age of Railways'.

It was an era which, as Bryan Morgan recalls in his introduction to the book *The Great Trains*, evokes a vision of "parasols at Biarritz, of huge portmanteaux at the Gare de l'Est bound for Baden-Baden, of winter-gardens and Fabergé jewels, of pink-shaded lights gleaming on the mahogany of the *wagon-restaurant,* of German bands and of garden-parties graced by boaters, blazers and picture-hats, of skies cloudless and untroubled save for the pioneering balloon, of 'summer journeys to Niagara' (and winter ones to Miami) in glistening green open-vestibuled Pullmans, of nabobs' and viceroys' private saloons on the *Poona Mail,* of Baedeker in its prime with the going easy . . ."

By 1890, the railway maps of the United Kingdom looked much the same as they do today. Locomotives, rolling stock and the technicalities of handling them had developed to the stage where speeds in excess of 70mph, combined with safety, were common, and the railways appeared to occupy a secure position as *the* popular means of mass travel. Nobody had yet evaluated the threats which would arise first from cheap personal transport in the form of the automobile and, later still, from the airways, putting flight within reach of the pockets of ordinary people.

At this stage, Britain held an easy lead over the rest of the world in railway operation. Figures compiled by Professor Foxwell and Lord Farrer, two leading authorities of the period, show that, in the late 1880s, the country where the railway originated could offer 62 904 miles of express running at an average speed, including stops, of 41.6mph.

The nearest rival in terms of mileage was northern Germany, a long way behind with 18 637 miles at 31.7mph. Next came the United States with 13 956 miles (the same average speed as in Britain) followed by France with 11 263 miles at 32.8mph. From there the list tails away to Italy with 1 213 miles at an average speed of 29.5mph.

The path immediately ahead lay with even higher speeds, allied to greater comfort and cheaper fares. In Britain, the Midland Railway, under its revered general manager, James Allport, had already led the way in pioneering a better deal for passengers.

The railways' popularity was never in doubt. In London, Liverpool Street Station on a summer afternoon would be packed with people going into the country for fishing, golf, tennis or picnics. There might be time to buy a book for the journey at Victoria Station (top).

Mary Evans

Radio Times Hulton

Legislation passed by Gladstone in 1844 had laid down that all railways should run at least one train a day which would call at all stations and carry third-class passengers in enclosed carriages at the statutory rate of a penny a mile. In 1872, the Midland decided to provide third-class accommodation on all its trains, including the fastest expresses, and in 1875 went a step further by abolishing its second class and opening these more comfortable coaches to the holders of third-class tickets. The company also reduced first-class fares to $1\frac{1}{2}$d a mile.

The notion that, if you provided better facilities at a lower cost, more people would travel by train and your revenue would increase, aroused criticism and hostility, both in the newspapers of the time and among rival railway companies. This was particularly true of the Great Northern and London & North Western after 1876 when the opening of the Midland line from Settle to Carlisle introduced a new claimant for Scottish traffic.

Racing to the North

Eventually, the Great Northern, which operated part of the eastern London–Edinburgh route, and the London & North Western, which provided a similar western service via Carlisle, decided to counterattack with speed. Their decision led to the thrilling *Races to the North* which captured the imagination of newspaper readers in the summer of 1888 with vivid reports.

The speed of the 10.00 expresses from King's Cross and Euston increased progressively until Edinburgh was reached at 17.27, 93 minutes ahead of schedule by the eastern route, and 17.38, 142 minutes ahead of schedule, by the western. These achievements are all the more impressive when one takes into account 20-minute stops at York and Preston for refreshments, neither express being equipped at the time with a restaurant car.

In the interests of safety, particularly in winter conditions, the standard times for the two journeys were eventually fixed at eight and a quarter hours and eight and a half hours respectively. Even so, the average speed in both cases was slightly over 47mph, a big advance on the schedules in force before the races showed what could be done.

The quest for speed after 1890 led to two further series of historic races — between London and Aberdeen in 1895, when the Great Northern and the London & North Western again entered into competition, the prize on this occasion being the growing Highland tourist traffic; and on the Plymouth–London run between 1904 and 1906 when the London & South Western and the Great Western engaged in a prestige struggle over the rapidity with which they could deliver transatlantic passengers and mails to the capital.

Several factors contributed to the stampede to the north in 1895 — the fact that Queen Victoria had put the Highlands on the map by spending her summer holiday at Balmoral . . . the popularity everywhere of Sir Walter Scott's novels . . . the shortening of the route to Aberdeen via the second Tay Bridge, the first having collapsed in the historic disaster of December 1879, and the magnificent Forth Bridge, opened by the Prince of Wales in March 1890.

Both the Great Northern and the London & North Western had continued their historic rivalry by running night tourist express trains to Aberdeen in the summer. Both trains departed from their respective London stations, King's Cross and Euston, at 20.00, but scheduled arrival times were different.

The Great Northern express, with a route 16 miles shorter, was due in at 07.35, while the London & North Western train was timed to arrive 15 minutes later. This scheduling made practical sense because, over the last 38 miles of the journey, both companies had to use the same stretch of Caledonian Railway from Kinnaber Junction, just north of Montrose, to Aberdeen.

In the summer of 1895 the London & North Western decided that arriving at 07.50 did not give passengers sufficient time to transfer masses of luggage to the local train for Ballater, timed to depart at 08.05. They therefore abandoned any pretence of running to time and simply tried to reach Aberdeen as fast as possible.

The outcome was several nights of madness in mid-August which made front page headlines, thrilled the public, treated passengers to bone-shaking rides and brought warnings that disaster must inevitably follow unless the madness ceased and some compromise was reached.

The Great Northern, having decided to establish its superiority by entering, if only briefly, a straightforward race, took a little time to match its rival's performance. On the night of August 20-21, however, less than a minute

separated the two expresses when they reached Kinnaber Junction.

The west coast train was still ahead on this occasion and eventually steamed into Aberdeen at 04.58, nearly three hours ahead of schedule, having averaged 60mph on the long haul from London. The position was reversed the next night when the east coast express triumphed easily, reaching Aberdeen at 04.40, and the owners came to the conclusion that they had proved their point and, in the interests of safety, should revert to normal running.

But the London & North Western was not prepared to let the matter rest there. Twenty-four hours later, the west coast express thundered through the night faster than ever to arrive at 04.32, eight minutes earlier again. The time for the run of 512 minutes represented an average speed of 63.3mph and set a record which still stands today.

One of the west coast locomotives involved in the races was the 2-4-0 *Hardwicke* which can be admired by visitors to the National Railway Museum at York. Although weighing only 35½ tons without its tender, the *Hardwicke* averaged 67.2mph for the 141 miles between Crewe and Carlisle, an astonishing performance considering that the route includes the 1:75 gradient over Shap Fell.

Enthusiasm for speed received a general setback the following summer, however, when one of the west coast expresses, hauled by two locomotives, was derailed on a curve after running through Preston far too fast. Thanks to the solid construction of the carriages, only one person was killed. Nevertheless, the public outcry which followed resulted in an end to the speed race and even in the slowing down of some express schedules which had hitherto been considered safe.

Four stages of the record breaking Race to the North in 1895 (below left to right): The West Coast train leaves No 8 platform, Euston, hauled by the three cylinder compound locomotive 'Adriatic' from London to Crewe. Mr Crooks was the driver on the Carlisle to Perth section; Mr Soutar then took over for the final run to Aberdeen, where he can be seen carried triumphantly on the shoulders of the crowd. The train had cut nearly three hours off the normal journey time! The Forth Bridge (below), opened in 1890, shortened the route to the North. The Great Northern carried freight, particularly bricks from Peterborough. This heavy freight locomotive was designed in 1901; its long boiler earned it the nickname Long Tom.

Illustrated London News

British Rail/Oxford Publishing Co.

It was much the same story — excitement, astounding performances, warnings of impending disaster, and, finally, a serious accident — when the Plymouth-London races began in 1904. At this period, many transatlantic liners, in the interests of time-saving for passengers, had begun to make Plymouth their first British port of call rather than Liverpool. Travellers on German ships also found they could reach their destination more quickly by disembarking at the Devon port, taking a train to London and completing their journey by one of the Channel ferries.

Two competing railway companies were involved, the London & South Western, which hauled the passengers, and the Great Western, which hauled the mails, and neither could resist the temptation to make a race of it.

The Great Western had just emerged from a decade of change and development. It had been forced to abandon Brunel's broad gauge, a move which necessitated the construction of 15 miles of sidings at Swindon as temporary accommodation for hundreds of locomotives, carriages and wagons which had to be converted to standard gauge, and the last broad gauge train had run on May 20, 1892.

Radio Times Hulton

The GWR remained a lively company, however, interested in improving its service and, in particular, achieving longer non-stop runs. In 1902 the eminent engineer, George Jackson Churchward, was placed in charge of the Swindon works and, the following year, produced a new class of locomotive, the 4-4-0 *City of Bath*, which received world-wide admiration for its technical improvements and efficiency.

On May 9, 1904, in the course of the Plymouth-London race, a locomotive of this class established what became known at the time as 'the record of records' although the speed actually achieved is still the subject of debate, among railway experts today. The events are dramatically described by Oswald Nock in his authoritative book *Railways Then and Now*:

"Two engines were involved in the record-breaking run. *City of Truro*, one of Churchward's new class, was the engine from Plymouth, and it was once through Exeter, with the sharply curved sections of the South Devon Line behind them, that the men on the *City of Truro* really began to pile it on.

"The 20-mile rise to Whiteball Tunnel was

covered at an average of 60mph, and then down the Wellington bank the engine was 'given her head'. Speeds leaped up until one very experienced recorder clocked a quarter-mile at 102.3mph; but . . . some platelayers were working on the line, and did not seem to realise how fast this 100-mph thunderbolt was bearing down on them.

"To a screaming fanfare on the whistle the brakes were applied, and all chances of

increasing speed or corroborating the record already secured was lost. That 102.3 will always be a point of controversy. The build-up towards it was rapid and continuous, with successive quarter-mile timings registering 81.8, 84.9, 88.2, 90.0, 91.8, 95.7 and 97.8mph.

"As an engineer I have analysed all the evidence and, although I too have doubts about the 102.3 for the final quarter, I would accept 100mph and perhaps a little over.

Letters for the north were actually sorted on the train, under bright gas lighting (far left). Standard gauge was finally established, the last train to use Brunel's broad gauge of 7ft 0¼ins was the 'Great Western', a single driver locomotive of the Iron Duke class, seen above leaving Paddington Station, London for its last journey to western Cornwall in 1892. The Great Western Railway's chief mechanical engineer from 1902 to 1921 was G. J. Churchward (centre). His advanced designs during this time put the Great Western in the forefront of

British locomotive engineering. Express passenger locomotive No 736 (below) was designed by Robert W. Urie of the London & South Western Railway. It was built at Eastleigh in 1918 and the design was slightly altered to become the Southern Railway's King Arthur class later, when it was christened 'Excalibur'.

"At Pylle Hill Junction — the engine-changing point in Bristol — the *City of Truro* was exchanged for the single-wheeler *Duke of Connaught,* and in the course of the run on to London the 70.3 miles from Shrivenham to Westbourne Park were covered in 52¾ minutes, an average of exactly *80mph.*

"Never previously had a train run at such speed continuously, over so long a distance, and it was truly said at the time that the men who rode in that travelled faster than man had ever done before, by any form of transport."

This second series of races came to an abrupt end on July 1, 1906 when the London & South Western boat train crashed on a curve outside Salisbury station, killing 24 passengers (mostly Americans), the driver, the fireman, and the fireman and guard of another train.

Victoria's Diamond Jubilee

As might be expected, nobody has ever travelled in greater luxury on British railways than members of the royal family. Queen Victoria was the first monarch to sample the then-new means of transport when, in 1842, she made the journey from Slough to Paddington in a luxurious saloon where the seats were Louis XIV-style hanging sofas of carved wood and the decorations included drapes of crimson-and-white silk and several exquisite paintings.

The Queen's comfort resulted in several 'firsts' for British railways. A London & Birmingham saloon used by her as early as 1843 was the first carriage with heating, provided by a small boiler under the floor; a GWR saloon built in 1850 had probably the first train lavatory in this country, plus a means of signalling to the driver whether to go faster or slow down; and, when the London & North Western Railway built two six-wheeled saloons — one for day travel, one for night — in 1869, they were connected by a bellows gangway, a precursor of corridor connections, introduced for the first time on an entire train in the United States in 1887.

The first royal train, as opposed to royal saloons, did not appear until ten years after that. In honour of the Queen's Diamond Jubilee in 1897, the GWR decided to spend £40 000 on a special train for exclusive royal use. The Queen, while accepting the gesture, stipulated that there was to be no question of

The SOUTHERN B
"One hour of luxurious
between

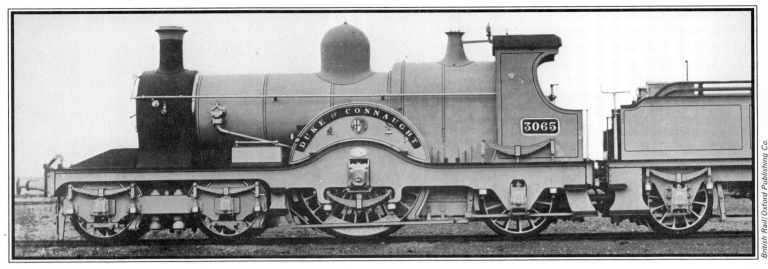

British Rail/Oxford Publishing Co.

British Rail

Illustrated London News

Radio Times Hulton

scrapping the Great Western saloon built for her 23 years earlier.

The saloon, still lit by oil lamps, was therefore incorporated in the six-coach train, which had gangway connections and electric lighting in the other carriages. Victoria travelled to Windsor and back in her beloved saloon when she celebrated her Diamond Jubilee there and the coach was also used to bring her coffin from Gosport to London when she died a little more than three years later.

Several examples of the luxury in which royalty travelled can be seen at York. They include two royal coaches — beautifully-designed 12-wheelers with silver-plated bedsteads, silver-plated baths and heavily-padded chairs and sofas — which the London & North Western built in 1903 for King Edward VII and Queen Alexandra. The craftsmanship and opulence are strongly evocative of an era of privilege soon to be shattered by the carnage and waste of the First World War.

While the ordinary traveller did not enjoy such lavish surroundings, a journey by rail had become a pleasure rather than a penance just before the turn of the century. Corridor trains with restaurant cars were common on long-distance expresses, and steam heat and electric light were being introduced.

Anyone willing to pay a supplement could also indulge in gracious living on wheels by travelling in one of the luxury coaches developed by the American, George Mortimer Pullman. The first meal on a British train was served in the Pullman coach *Victoria* in 1874.

One of the great champions of Pullman travel was the future Lord Dalziel, ex-journalist, ex-taxi owner and an astute financier who, when he turned his energies to the railways, pioneered the *Southern Belle*, an all-Pullman train, which made the 51 miles between London and Brighton in an hour.

He was also responsible for the negotiations which, ten years after the death of George Mortimer Pullman, resulted in the separation of the British and American Pullman companies in 1907. One immediate result was the abandonment of the overall brown colour which had been the Pullman trademark up to this time. As Bryan Morgan explains in one of his contributions to *The Great Trains:*

"Dalziel's company adopted a splendid livery of umber and cream adorned with a royal-looking heraldic device; but it retained its parent's pleasant custom of christening individual cars, and together with such touches as scented soap tablets and white-gloved attendants this endured even after its nationalisation in 1962 and right up to the withdrawal of those traditional saloons which had approached two hundred in number."

The *Southern Belle,* later renamed the *Brighton Belle,* was only one of many fine trains which carried passengers to their destinations in speed and comfort and have earned themselves an enduring place in British railway history.

GWR's 'City of Truro' reached the astonishing speed of 100mph in 1904, hauling an ocean mail special to Bristol; the train was taken over by the 'Duke of Connaught', which averaged 71.5mph up to London. Coaches built for King Edward and Queen Alexandra in 1903 (left) had the most luxurious 'day saloon' (circled).
The 'Brighton Belle' was an all-Pullman train. Her first-class passengers travelled in well-upholstered luxury in the Pullman car 'Alberta'. (centre).

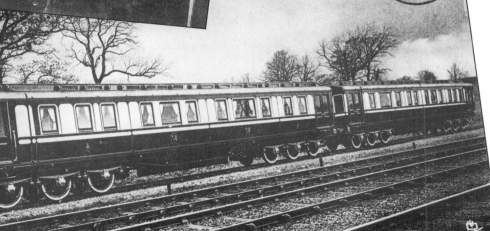

The *Irish Mail* left Euston each night at 20.45, bound for Holyhead and the steamer connection to Dublin. A few minutes before the doors were shut, a postman would appear carrying a leather pouch containing a watch, set at Greenwich Mean Time. The watch was handed over to the postmaster aboard the train so that 'The King's Time' might be delivered to Dublin next morning.

With the coming of radio time signals after the First World War, it was no longer necessary to send the time to Dublin. Nevertheless, the Euston ceremony was carried out solemnly each night although the watch, having been delivered and signed for, was carried only as far as Holyhead. To the regret of traditionalists, the custom was finally abandoned in 1939.

The final great railway construction of the Victorian era – the line linking Manchester and London via Sheffield, Nottingham and Leicester, a project of the Manchester, Sheffield & Lincolnshire Railway – was widely attacked on economic grounds for already critics had nicknamed the M.S.&L. – 'Money Sunk and Lost.' Further acrimony arose when it was learned that it was proposed to build a new London terminus which would be reached by tunnelling under Lord's cricket ground.

Despite all the objections, the scheme was forced through by Sir Edward Watkin, one of the last great characters of the railway age, who felt himself hemmed in by rival companies, and, as a leading supporter of the construction of a Channel tunnel, envisaged the day when through trains would run from Manchester to Paris over his tracks.

He changed the name of the company to the Great Central ('G.C. or Gone Completely' as the financial critics put it) and London's last, and smallest, main line terminus, Marylebone, was formally opened on March 9, 1899. This development necessitated moving headquarters to London, a move which had a mixed reception with many of the staff. In a kindly thought designed to overcome reluctance to make the change, the company bought a plot of land in Ardwick Cemetery and announced that anyone making the transfer to the capital would be brought back to Manchester at the end of his days and be buried there free of charge!

From 1904 travellers to the West Country could enjoy the longest non-stop run in the world – 245 miles from Paddington to Plymouth. Two years later, with completion of a new direct line through Taunton, plus the introduction of corridor stock, came the birth of the GWR express, the *Cornish Riviera Limited.*

The express was scheduled to leave Paddington at 10.30 hours, a departure time that was to remain unchanged for nearly 70 years, and reach Plymouth, 226 miles away, four hours later. There were two interesting innovations designed to increase the comfort of *third-class* passengers. A valet was available to clean the shoes of the gentlemen while a maid, dressed in nurse's uniform, was available for the ladies. Her duties included patrolling the corridors and keeping a specially careful watch 'over ladies travelling without an escort.' Such facilities were not, of course, needed by first-class passengers who, it was assumed, would travel with their own entourage of servants.

Continental links

Continental travel became increasingly popular – the first day excursion to Calais had been arranged in 1888 – and five of the leading British railway companies ran their own cross-Channel ferries: Dover-Calais (London, Chatham & Dover), Folkestone-Boulogne (South Eastern), Newhaven-Dieppe (London, Brighton & South Coast), Southampton-Le Havre (London & South Western) and, for a time, Weymouth-Cherbourg (Great Western).

Although the French had introduced a 900-ton, screw-driven ship on the Newhaven-Dieppe route by that time, British cross-Channel services relied until 1890 on paddle-steamers, capable of 20 knots, but small and cramped. In that year, the London & South Western switched to a 1000-ton, twin-screw vessel. The next major development was the appearance in 1902 of the 1650-ton *Queen,* plying between Dover and Calais at 21¾ knots.

Before the decade was out, the Belgians had introduced the triple-screw turbine ferry *Princess Elizabeth* (1747 tons, 24 knots) between Dover and Ostend, and the French were operating a similar vessel of 1882 tons on the Newhaven-Dieppe route. However, these ships were not exactly monsters if you

compare them with the latest 5600-ton British Rail car ferries, and a Channel crossing on a bad day or night remained a daunting prospect until long after 1920.

The tiny ships were ill-equipped to cope with the force of a Channel gale while passengers had to make do with a choice between small, stuffy saloons where they were surrounded by vomiting fellow-passengers, or freezing on decks which offered little protection against wind or rain. The misery of such a journey was captured graphically by Evelyn Waugh in his novel *Vile Bodies,* published as late as 1930:

"Sometimes the ship pitched and sometimes she rolled and sometimes she stood quite still and shivered all over, poised above an abyss of dark water; then she would go swooping down like a scenic railway train into a windless hollow and up again with a rush into the gale; sometimes she would burrow her path, with convulsive nosings and scramblings like a terrier in a rabbit hole; and sometimes she would drop dead like a lift. It was this last movement that caused the most havoc among the passengers.

" 'Oh,' said the Bright Young People, 'Oh, oh, oh.'

" 'It's just exactly like being inside a cocktail shaker,' said Miles Malpractice. 'Darling, your face – eau de Nil.'

" 'Too, too sick-making,' said Miss Runcible, with one of her rare flashes of accuracy . . .

"To Father Rothschild no passage was worse than any other. He thought of the suffering of the saints, the mutability of human nature, the Four Last Things, and between whiles repeated snatches of the penitential psalms . . .

"The ship creaked in every plate, doors slammed, trunks fell about, the wind howled; the screw, now out of the water, now in, raced and churned, shaking down hat boxes like ripe apples . . .''

The obvious cure for so much suffering was a Channel tunnel but experimental work had been abandoned by the Board of Trade in 1882, largely on grounds of national security. The matter was the subject of debate again in 1906 and 1913, but the isolationists repeated their earlier victory.

By the turn of the century, a number of factors were contributing to the substantial

increase in train weight. Steel had begun to replace wood for carriage construction; continuous-braking systems meant that heavier loads could be hauled at speed without the dangers which had caused so many accidents in the past; and the demands of passengers for greater comfort did nothing to reduce overall weight. Heavier trains meant bigger, or more efficient, locomotives, or possibly a combination of both concepts.

In the United States, where the quality of coal was inferior, the emphasis was initially on sheer size — bigger boilers and bigger grates, which led to development of the 4-4-2 *Atlantic* and 4-6-2 *Pacific* locomotives. Europe contributed two innovations which were important in terms of increased efficiency. Compounding — using the same steam, first in high-pressure cylinders, then in low-pressure — was perfected in France, having first been tried in Britain and the United States. Germany, for its part, invented superheating of steam, which increased locomotive power considerably.

Britain tended, by and large, to ignore these developments and stick to the economical, but effective, 4-4-0 locomotives, which had spread across the world after first appearing in the United States in the 1840s, and, in the second half of the century, hauled most of the world's passenger trains.

Oswald Nock says in his book *Railways Then and Now:* "In the year 1906 one could move around the main line railways of Great Britain and on 15 of them see this remarkable medium-powered passenger type in a variety of lineaments, in a far greater variety of

liveries, but all roughly within the 50- to 60-ton range.

"All were little masterpieces of artistic symmetry; all were the pride and joy of the men who ran them. But with very few exceptions they were leading the locomotive practice of their owners into a blind alley, from which the vastly changed economic circumstances of the 1920s were to block nearly every single road of escape.

"The Great Western was the only British railway on which a really far-sighted plan of development was evolving in the first decade of the twentieth century. Churchward was planning for the future, and always considered that the boiler constituted the principal problem of the steam locomotive, and in 1908, furthering all the features he had so far developed, he built a huge engine, the first British *Pacific* . . .

"But Churchward's engine, *The Great Bear,* was vastly in advance of its time so far as Great Britain was concerned, and his much smaller four-cylinder 4-6-0s of the *Star* class, weighing no more than 75.6 tons and having a grate area of 27 square feet, proved amply adequate for the most severe demands of everyday traffic, until the year 1923 . . ."

The failure of British companies to embark enthusiastically on the development of the new and more powerful locomotives that would inevitably be needed was partly a question of tradition, partly of economics.

Britain, with plenty of good quality coal, had always relied on small, efficient and economic locomotives to haul its expresses. Custom was therefore a strong barrier to

change and the mood was reinforced by the economic climate of the Edwardian era. Coal was becoming more expensive; wages were rising; social and political unrest had begun to appear. All of these trends affected the railways, which were among the biggest employers of labour in the country.

Furthermore, they had just started to feel the pinch from rival forms of transport, particularly the electric train and the automobile. In the circumstances, it is not surprising that there was considerable resistance to schemes involving heavy capital investment, and the matter was finally rendered — for the time being — academic with the outbreak of the First World War.

Sir Edward Watkin, chairman of South Eastern Railways from 1866 to 1894, keenly supported plans for the Channel tunnel. Although these failed, South East & Chatham launched the cross-Channel steamer, the turbine-powered 'Queen', in 1902 (opposite). She was lost in action in 1916.
In 1898 the Great Northern Railway introduced the 'Atlantic' locomotive (top left), the pair of trailing wheels supporting a larger fire box. It was later called 'Henry Oakley'.
The Wolverton works (above) produced coaches for the London & North Western Railway; here the chassis is lowered onto the bogies. Because of its size the giant locomotive 'The Great Bear' (below) was only used on the London to Bristol line.

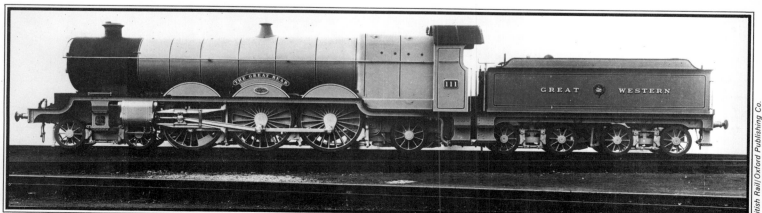

British locomotives, and the men who drove them, did heroic work throughout the war when they faced competition for fuel from the Royal Navy's coal-fired battleships; when servicing facilities were vastly reduced because railway plants had been switched to munitions manufacture; and when the tonnage of trains reached limits unheard of in peacetime.

After 1916, these problems combined to bring about a general reduction in speeds. For passengers, the chief wartime discomforts arose from the general withdrawal of restaurant cars, except on the Great Central, and the widespread use of non-corridor carriages because they were lighter.

Nobody suffered greater hardship on the railways than sailors bound for Scapa Flow, which had been chosen as the main base of the Grand Fleet because of its strategic position. A train for service personnel, known as the *Jellicoe Special,* left Euston at 15.00 hours each day on the 700-mile journey to Thurso in the north of Scotland, via Carlisle, Inverkeithing (for Rosyth, the naval base on the Forth) and Perth. The scheduled time was 27¾ hours, but the trip sometimes took four days if there was snow on the line.

In the mid-1960s, Malcolm Brown and Patricia Meehan advertised for reminiscences about Scapa Flow when they were making a BBC TV documentary about the Orkney anchorage. They received hundreds of letters in reply, many of them from men who still bore the scars of those miserable railway journeys undertaken half a century earlier.

Three examples from the book *Scapa Flow,* compiled by Mr Brown and Miss Meehan from the letters sent to them, read:

"The memory I have was of being confined to the train and living on pies for about three days, with an occasional wash by putting our heads out of the railway carriage window to catch the raindrops."

"Men, bags, baggage of all descriptions everywhere, including kitbags and hammocks and the inevitable assortment of 'empties'. In the afternoon, and more particularly at night, the train was strewn with 'bodies' trying to sleep.

"The air was dense with smoke and smelt more like a ship's bilges than a train; but the thought of having a window open, even if one could get to it, was out of the question and asking for trouble. Little or no heat was provided by the train and it was a case of putting up with any discomfort to keep warm."

The third correspondent found himself and a number of companions in the unusual position of having a service-woman as a

travelling companion, he recalled:

"It was not long before nature began to assert itself . . . As I was sitting next to the young lady, I was given several nudges and whispers which put me in a predicament, but the situation was saved by the young lady herself who, after first telling me she had been travelling all day from France and fully understood the position, said she would read her newspaper for a few minutes, which she did and soon everyone was relieved and comfortable."

Another matter shelved because of the war was the quest for greater railway safety. The standard was already high in Britain. All signals and points on passenger lines were interlocked and the running of trains was regulated by the block system, which stopped a driver from proceeding unless the section of track ahead of him was clear.

NORTH WESTERN RAILWAY.

NOTICE TO STAFF.

The Government has decided to take over the control of the Railways of Great Britain in connection with the Mobilization of the Troops and general movements in connection with Naval & Military requirements. The management of the Railway and the existing terms of employment of the staff will remain unaltered, and all instructions will be issued through the same channels as heretofore.

Euston Station,
August, 1914.

ROBERT TURNBULL,
General Manager.

There was, however, still the factor of human error. The failure of a driver to read signals correctly led to a dramatic crash in Westmorland in September 1913 when one sleeping-car express from Carlisle ran into the back of another, causing many casualties. But it was not until after the war, in 1920, that the introduction of colour-light signals, so bright that they could be seen a mile away on a sunny day, on the Liverpool Overhead Railway, pointed the way to the modern signalling system that enables 100-mph expresses to be run on the same tracks at five-minute intervals.

Despite all the amalgamations which had taken place over a period of nearly a century, Britain was still served by well over a hundred separate railway companies at this time with sometimes as many as seven or eight of them serving places like Carlisle, Cardiff and Manchester.

In the rumbustious years since 1825, they had had a powerful influence on the way of life of everyone in the country. They owned docks (the GWR was the largest single dock-owner in the country), 70 hotels and steamers. They had been responsible for the creation of new ports (Barry, Immingham) and new towns (Crewe, New Swindon), which were important railway construction centres as well as important junctions.

They endowed institutes, hospitals, clubs and churches (one Welsh company advised its staff 'to attend a place of worship on Sundays as this will be a means of promotion when vacancies occur'), and the larger companies were the biggest employers of labour in the country apart from the Post Office.

But, when the troops came home and the world turned to reconstruction after the Great War, the sun was already going down on The Golden Age of Railways in Britain and the distant-signals were set at danger. Ahead lay amalgamation, decline and, eventually, nationalization.

The Government took over control of the Railways in 1914 for the war (see poster above). Railway stations all over Europe resembled this scene at Victoria Station, London (left).

FRANCE GATHERS MC

The coming of the railway aroused the same mixture of emotions in France as it had in England. On the one hand there were those who regarded it as one of humanity's madder excesses, both noisy and uncomfortable, and caricaturists mocked the whole notion of travel, depicting, for example, well-heeled voyagers making the journey to Rocquefort to buy some of the famous cheese which was available just as readily from their neighbourhood grocers at home.

On the other, there were men like Pierre Larousse, compiler of the famous French encyclopedia, who felt instinctively the romance of the 'iron horse' and foresaw what a difference it would make to the lives of ordinary men and women. "Railway!" he wrote. "A magical aura already surrounds the word; it is a synonym for civilization, progress and fraternity. Up to now man had gazed at the denizens of the air and of the sea with envy and a certain feeling of inferiority; thanks to the railway, the birds and fish no longer have an advantage over him."

France had its first steam locomotives for industrial lines from Robert Stephenson & Company in 1828. The following year, Marc Seguin built an experimental locomotive in France, and the country's first public steam railway was the Paris & Saint-Germain, opened as far as Le Pecq in 1837. Other local lines followed, and one international trunk route from Strasbourg to Basle in Switzerland was completed in 1841.

Thomas Crampton evolved his locomotive in England, but it proved much more popular in France and Germany, where it was used on express trains. First built in 1846, it had large diameter driving wheels right at the back. This model was built for the Northern Railway in France in 1859, but is shown here as it was in the 1880s, after the vacuum brake had been fitted and a cab provided for the engineman.

MENTUM

From the start France favoured a national plan for railways. The above lines were built under a law of 1833 which laid down the principle that all railways should belong to the state and companies could have no more than a lease of the 'infrastructure' – the works and buildings – for a period of 99 years.

Another law of 1842 outlined the national trunk routes for which companies could compete in offers for the lease once the state had built the infrastructure. These trunk routes became the main arteries of the great French railway companies, usually formed through a merger of smaller lines and given a monopoly in their territory. They included the Paris-Orleans, a local railway which gained the south-west concession in 1843; the Eastern Railway and the Northern Railway, both based in Paris, which were formed in 1845; the Midi Railway, based on a cross-country route from Bordeaux to Sète on the Mediterranean, founded in 1852; and the Western Railway of 1853. There was also the great Paris, Lyons & Mediterranean Railway, which was the result of a merger of smaller lines in 1857 and six years later leaped across the sea to extend its operations to Algeria.

Slow start

These dates suggest that, despite the enthusiasm of men like Larousse, railways got off to a comparatively slow start in France. This was the case. By 1850 the country had only 1927 miles of railway compared with 9072 in the United States, 6658 in the United Kingdom and 3777 in Germany.

The French difficulty was lack of capital, engineering know-how and skilled workers in these early years. Britain made up all three deficiencies at the start. Two-thirds of the money to build the Paris-Rouen line, which opened in May 1843, came from Britain; the engineer who planned it was British (Joseph Locke); and the contractors who did the work were British (Thomas Brassey and William Mackenzie).

To build the 82-mile line (later part of the Western Railway), which involved four bridges across the Seine and four tunnels, one more than a mile and a half long, through hard limestone, Brassey and Mackenzie hired 5000 British navvies to work alongside – and set an example to – 5000 men of other nationalities.

The British navvies astonished the natives by their prodigious appetite for beef, brandy and hard work. The French made pilgrimages just to watch them wielding their picks and shovels. Locke said: "Often have I heard the exclamation of French loungers around a group of navvies, '*Mon Dieu, ces Anglais, comme ils travaillent!*'"

Many navvies stayed on, married French women and worked on other Brassey contracts – the 58-mile Rouen-Le Havre extension, begun in 1843; Amiens-Boulogne (1844); Rouen-Dieppe (1847) – when the Paris-Rouen line was finished. The Rouen-Le Havre route proved particularly difficult; involving tunnels, bridges and an enormous viaduct, 100 feet high with 27 arches, at Barentin, 12 miles from Rouen.

The viaduct, which had been put up with poor lime in wet weather, collapsed on January 10, 1846, when it was almost com-

BPC

plete, bringing violent newspaper attacks on the French directors of the company and the shoddy workmanship of the foreigners they employed. Brassey salvaged his reputation by rebuilding the viaduct in six months at a cost of £40 000. "I have contracted to make and maintain the road, and nothing shall prevent Thomas Brassey from being as good as his word," he told the company. And, by 1848, he and his partners could claim to have built, largely with British capital, 75 per cent of France's railways.

From that time to 1890 the French network grew steadily with around 475 miles of new line being added every year until it reached three-quarters of the maximum total of more than 25000 miles. Amalgamation of seven of the largest companies took place in 1850, and, in 1878, the government took over a number of railways in the west of the country which were in financial difficulties, thus adding a state element to the existing system.

Metric gauge

British influence dictated that the gauge of the earliest French railways was 4ft 8½in which, in Continental terms, worked out at 1435mm. Someone in France noted that, if the gauge was measured between the vertical axes of the rails, a much tidier figure of 1500mm was the result, and this led to what may be called the 'French gauge aberration'.

The French took to quoting the 1500mm figure as standard gauge. True gauge then depended on the shape of the railhead, and, once this had been more or less standardized, the French found they had a true gauge of 1445mm. The 10mm difference did not interfere with through-working of rolling stock, however, and it is only in this century that France, by international agreement, has returned to the original British gauge of 1435mm, but Algeria (first railway, 1862) and Tunisia (1874), whose tracks were French-built, retain the 1445mm gauge to this day.

The arrival of French railways on the north coast of France inspired a dream which is still very much alive today – the building of a Channel tunnel. The idea was not even then new. As early as 1802, before the dawn of the Railway Age, a French mining engineer named Mathieu had suggested the idea to

France's first steam locomotive was built by Marc Seguin (left) in 1829. He also engineered France's first modern suspension bridge and railway tunnels. Thomas Brassey (far right), the great railway contractor, first worked as a quarryman on the Liverpool & Manchester Railway. By 1848, his company had built 75 per cent of the French rail system. The Rouen-Le Havre route presented enormous challenges, particularly in the construction of the viaduct at Barentin (right). British navvies were regarded as astonishingly hard workers – and drinkers! Below right a group of them are seen celebrating the opening of the Paris-Rouen line in 1843.

Napoleon, who was sufficiently enthusiastic to say to the British ambassador in Paris: "This is one of the great things we ought to do together."

The subsequent wars led to the scheme being put aside and forgotten, and British suspicions about French intentions – the Duke of Wellington even opposed the building of the London-Folkestone line on military grounds – ensured that it remained shelved for fifty years.

Plans were then drawn up for a £120 million tunnel to be built at depths of 60 to 100 feet beneath the seabed. Work did not actually begin, however, until 1881 when trial borings were made, starting near Calais and Dover and eventually reaching a mile under the Channel on each side. A machine was used which had a drilling head seven feet in diameter, worked by compressed air, and was capable of boring 18 yards a day.

Renewed tension between the two countries when Britain occupied Egypt and obtained control of the Suez Canal in the 1880s led to Parliament deciding by 222 votes to 84 that boring should cease on the British side. It was to be 80 years, by which time the estimated cost had soared to £1000 million, before the scheme was seriously considered again in a climate of European unity. The old borings were found to be in good condition and, although unlined, had admitted very little water.

Crossing the frontiers

But, whatever the fears of governments, international travel by rail became an increasing reality from the earliest years. France was early linked with Belgium through the Belgian State Railway – the world's first planned trunk railway system – which had a north-south route from Antwerp to Mons and a west-east route from Ostend to the German border near Aachen. The initial section from Brussels north to Malines was opened in 1835, the first public steam railway on the Continent, and the complete network of nearly 350 miles of railway was finished in 1843.

Strasbourg, as already mentioned, was connected with Basle in Switzerland by a French line (later part of the Eastern Railway) which opened in 1841, and, in 1857, largely through Italian vision backed by Italian capital, work

began on the first great Alpine tunnel at Mont Cenis (also known as the Fréjus tunnel). This was designed to open up a direct route between Paris and Turin, Milan and the rich Lombardy plain.

The route involved a bore of 8 miles 868 yards under the Alps. In the early 1860s it was not expected that this tunnel would be completed for another 14 years or so, as drilling holes to blast with gunpowder was an extremely slow process and gunpowder itself had limited blasting power.

Blasting power

Two inventions — the pneumatic drill, by the Frenchman, Germain Sommeiller in 1862, and Alfred Nobel's much more powerful dynamite, first used at Mont Cenis in 1867 — led to a great quickening of the work, and, despite the distractions of the Franco-Prussian war, the tunnel opened for traffic on September 17, 1871. It was, incidentally, the news that the tunnellers were using compressed air from tubes more than half a mile long which gave George Westinghouse the idea of a compressed-air brake linking every coach of a train with the locomotive.

The following year, the coastal route linking France with Italy — through Nice and Monte Carlo — was completed to the frontier town of Ventimiglia. It extended a holiday area which had been popular with the leisured English classes since the late eighteenth century — in the 1860s, according to one writer, there were more English than French in Nice. Both Britain and France also used the

The No. 390 'Balzac' (below) is a modified version of the Engerth locomotive, built in 1856 for the Northern Railway in France. The tender was articulated to the main frame so that part of its weight rested on the engine's rear driving wheels. The additional weight increased the engine's adhesion to the rails, and thus heavy freight trains could haul far heavier loads. In practice the advantages were outweighed by the extra cost and complication of the articulation. Anatole Mallet devised the first successful compound locomotive, used on the Bayonne-Biarritz Railway in 1876 (right). In compound working steam is used in one cylinder and then the other.

La Vie du Rail

Mont Cenis route to speed communications with their possessions in India.

This was not a new idea. As early as 1855 French railways ran a mail-only train called the *Malle des Indes* which connected Calais with Marseilles where the mail was loaded on liners bound for the Far East. For Britain, in particular, it meant a saving of several days in the despatch and receipt of documents and letters.

High-speed mail

A further saving was made from 1869 by using the Mont Cenis route to link up with ships calling at the Adriatic port of Brindisi. Just how important this saving was considered to be is indicated by the fact that, until the actual tunnel was completed two

years later, the mail was carried over the summit of the pass on a temporary, narrow-gauge track.

Passengers were allowed on the train in 1880 and, in 1890, it was split into two parts, the passenger section being known as *The Peninsular Express*. You left London at 15.15 on a Friday, arrived in Paris at 23.00, left Paris at 00.15 on the Saturday morning and reached Brindisi at 16.00 on Sunday afternoon. The old Marseilles service was also revived as *The Bombay Express* and ran until the outbreak of the Second World War.

On the Continent, as in Britain, you had to be an emperor or an empress, a king or a queen, before you had a hope of being provided with such facilities as a proper bed or a lavatory on a train before 1870. The man

who made the major contribution towards changing that situation — as well as making international rail travel easier and more comfortable — was Georges Nagelmackers, founder of the legendary *Compagnie Internationale des Wagons-Lits et des Grands Express Européens.*

Nagelmackers, a Belgian engineer who had been inspired by the achievements of George Mortimer Pullman in persuading more than a hundred American railroads to haul his luxury coaches, decided to try to apply the same system to European travel.

He had five sleeping cars built in Vienna to his design. They were four-wheelers, 29ft 3in long. In each car was a centre compartment containing lavatory facilities connected with three other compartments which

Wagons-Lits Company

BPC

could be used as a sitting room by day and converted into a comfortable bedroom by night.

Initially, he hoped to attach them to the *Malle des Indes* train between France and Brindisi. The railway companies refused to cooperate, however, after a government warning that they would be expected to charge less for hauling the mail if they were also providing a passenger service with the same train. At the end of 1872, therefore, a disappointed but still-optimistic Nagelmackers put his sleepers into service on three other routes, Paris-Cologne, Ostend-Berlin and Vienna-Munich.

Lack of customers was his chief trouble — no sensible person believed that it was possible to sleep normally on a train — until he opened the Paris-Vienna service in time for the exhibition there in 1873. Shortage of capital hindered development, however, and he also found himself facing an attempt by Pullman to establish his company on the Continent.

Sleeping partner

The situation forced Nagelmackers into a temporary alliance with Colonel William d'Alton Mann, Pullman's mini-rival in the United States. His company was re-named Mann's Railway Sleeping Carriage Company Limited, registered in London, and soon there were 16 Mann Boudoir Sleeping Cars running on the Continent.

The growing success of the service enabled Nagelmackers to raise enough capital in 1876 to buy MRSC's 22 contracts to operate on Continental railways, together with the total stock of sleeping cars, which had risen to 53. The purchase was made in the name of a new 11 million-franc company which Nagelmackers had formed in Paris, the *Compagnie Internationale des Wagons-Lits*, one day to become synonymous with luxury rail travel throughout Europe. It was also one of the first international corporations, at home in any country, and in its time was to serve three continents.

The main barriers to smooth international travel over long distances at this time were the need to stop periodically so that passengers could eat, and the wearying delays at frontier customs' posts. Nagelmackers next set about solving both of these problems.

In 1881, after design experiments, he ordered the first of his wagon-restaurants, whose culinary standards were to become a byword, from the Munich firm of Rathgeber. The carriage was a six-wheeler — some railways still refused to accept American-style bogie carriages because they feared they were unstable — which was capable of seating 12 diners at a time at tables for two or four.

The chairs and walls were padded with Spanish leather, the ceiling was Italian-style stucco, the cooking was done on a coal-fired range, and the car was lit by gas, carried in two cylinders. Tried out for a year on the Marseilles-Nice run, the wagon-restaurant proved a great success.

And so to Asia

Over the question of frontier delays, Nagelmackers decided they could best be overcome by having sealed luggage compartments, whose contents could be examined on arrival, and by arranging for hand baggage to be examined during the journey. The result was the departure of the first all-*Wagons-Lits* company train from Paris to Vienna on the evening of October 10, 1882.

The train, which weighed just over 100 tons and consisted of three six-wheel sleepers, a bogie sleeper and a diner (with half the axles of the coaches unbraked), covered the 884 miles (1414 kilometres) on the outward journey in 27hrs 53mins, an average speed of just over 30mph (48 km/h), and cut more than three hours from the normal running time. An almost identical speed was achieved on the return journey.

This trial run suggested that it might be possible to reduce the time of the journey from Paris to Constantinople, gateway to Asia, by as much as a day and a half. Thus was born the most famous and most romantic of all the great European expresses, the *Orient Express*. The train made its first journey on June 5, 1883. There was no fanfare attached to the departure, however, because new bogie sleeping cars, which were gaining increasing acceptance, had not been delivered on time.

The official inauguration did not therefore take place until October 4 of that year when, in honour of the occasion, to the name of the company on the side of the new coaches were added the words, '*et des Grands*

Express Européens'. At this time the *Orient Express* ran only as far as Bucharest, via Munich, Vienna and Budapest, and Constantinople could be reached — in a total journey time of 80 hours — by taking a steamer down the Danube or by local train and a ship across the Black Sea.

From June 1, 1889, however, it became possible to make the direct journey from Paris to Constantinople when Budapest in Hungary became linked with Turkey by completion of the line through Belgrade and Niš to Sofia in Bulgaria in 1888. This reduced the time of the journey to 67hrs 35mins.

In his book *Grand European Expresses*, George Behrend tells the story that opening up of the direct route is said to have involved obtaining the personal signature of Prince Ferdinand of Bulgaria, born a German prince. Nagelmackers sent one of his lieutenants, Vicomte de Richemont, to Sofia where the emissary found that he could not see the Prince unless he wore a court uniform.

He did not have any kind of uniform with him. "But," says Mr Behrend, "he obtained an audience of Ferdinand by appearing as a captain of the Prince's own police, whereupon Ferdinand is said to have exclaimed: 'What a ridiculous country!' "

Conspiracy and seduction

The *Orient Express* has inspired the fertile imagination of many an author. High-class courtesans sway down its corridors . . . corpses drip blood . . . beautiful spies seduce secret messengers . . . drugs are concealed in mysterious places. As far as is known, however, the only time the train has needed more than routine police attention was in 1891 when Macedonian partisans kidnapped four Germans and held them to ransom.

The famous *Blue Train*, another of Nagelmackers's creations, is almost as old as the *Orient Express*. It began its career on December 8, 1883 as the Calais-Nice-Rome express. The *Sud Express*, linking Lisbon with Paris and Calais, ran for the first time on November 4, 1887. In 1888, when an exclusive Pullman contract to operate in northern Italy ran out, Nagelmackers also planned a new *Rome Express*, using the more direct Mont Cenis route.

Sleeping cars from Calais and Paris, plus ordinary coaches, opened the new service

The great Wagons-Lits Company was founded by the Belgian engineer Georges Nagelmackers (far left). Needing extra capital at first he joined forces with the dubious American Colonel d'Alton Mann, seen standing (left) by one of their boudoir cars in 1874. The Wagons-Lits interiors (below) had sleeping compartments, which converted into comfortable day time space, and compact lavatories. The dining cars in the 1880s were sumptuous, with Spanish leather on the walls and stuccoed ceilings. Not only were passengers well fed, their feet were warmed with cosy 'bouillottes' (right), although the lighting was still smoky oil lamps, renewed at main stations (far right).

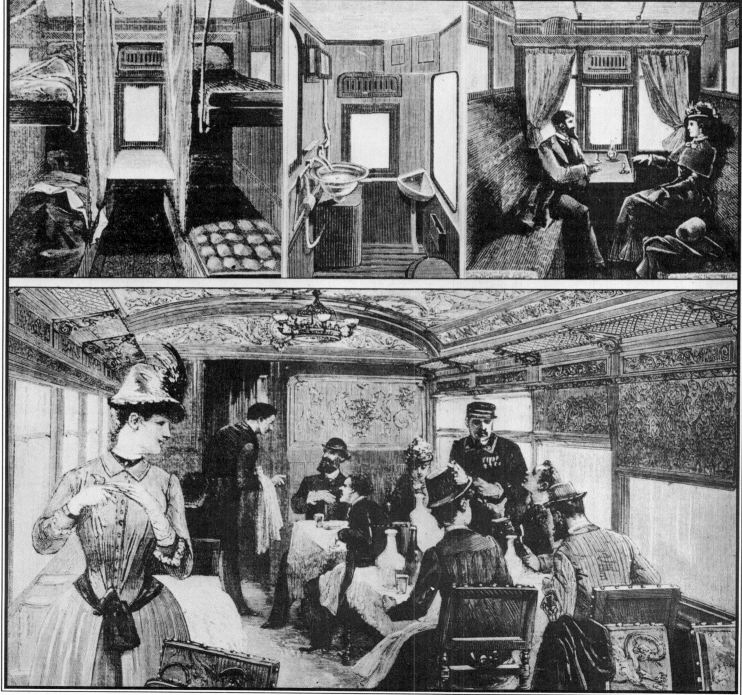

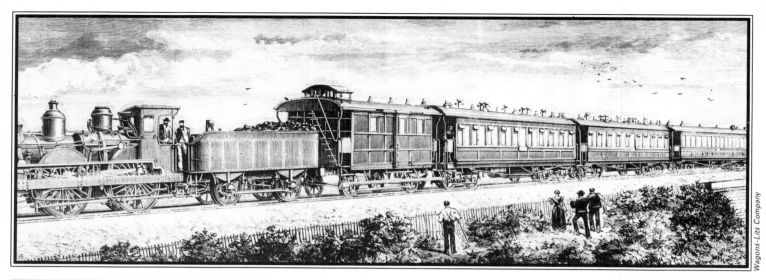

The most famous and romantic of all trains was the 'Orient Express' (left). At first the 'Express' ran only as far as Bucharest, and the journey to Constantinople had to be completed by boat across the Black Sea. From 1889 the direct route by rail was opened, with a journey of 67hr 35min, for which Nagelmackers could take much of the credit.

Before the restaurant car was introduced, passengers on French railways had to rush wildly for the station buffet at stops (below). The Wagons-Lits Company brought a high standard of cuisine to railway passengers in their dining cars, as this menu shows (right).

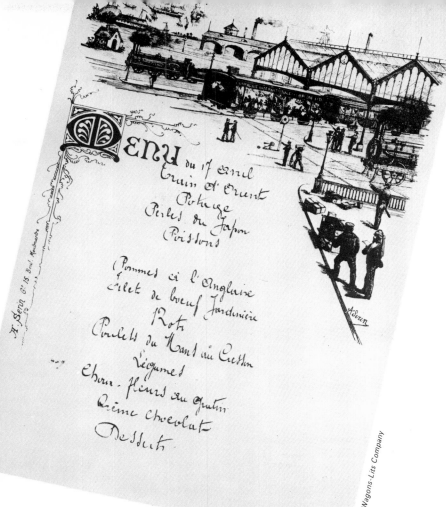

on November 15, 1890 over the Aix-les-Bains, Turin, Genoa, Pisa line with connections to Florence and Naples. In the meantime, the energetic and persuasive Belgian had entered Britain as well to challenge his Pullman rivals there. *Wagons-Lits,* using its own coaches, began a special fast service from London to Paris, via Dover and Calais, in 1889.

The service, which was called *The Club Train,* ran under a contract with the London, Chatham & Dover Railway, which had laid on a fast packetboat, the *Calais-Douvres.* Times were further cut by allowing only five minutes to transfer from train to ship and back again at the ports. The service proved popular in its inaugural year, which coincided with the Paris Exhibition, but the British company, having lost £20 000 on *The Club Train* in the previous 12 months, broke the contract in 1883 and Nagelmackers lost his slender foothold in Britain.

The *de luxe* standards provided by Nagelmackers's private company were not yet matched by the railway companies' own services, and neither money nor position could guarantee a comfortable journey, even on a popular route. The Baroness de Stoeckl, a kinswoman of the British royal family, has given this account of a journey in search of Mediterranean sunshine which she undertook in 1886:

"All went well until we arrived at Calais where, as usual, there was a wild rush for the buffet as in those days there were no restaurant cars on the trains. Everybody ordered the same: *Un potage, un demi-poulet, pommes purées, un demi de vin rouge.* We only had 25 minutes in which to eat this . . .

"Waiters flew frantically in every direction, at last came the cry, *'Dans cinq minutes le train part pour Paris.'* Then a general rush, *garçons* making out *les additions,* the travellers trying to finish, the *demi-poulet* and at the same time struggling into their coats, picking up bags, etc. . . . Then running like maniacs along the platform, maids with anxious faces pointing to the various compartments . . .

"There were no lavatories and no corridors; most people took with them a most useful domestic utensil, the emptying of which necessitated the frequent lowering of the window."

After changing in Paris for the 18-hour journey to Nice, the Baroness found herself in a compartment which "consisted of three large seats with padded backs, these had a handle which one pulled and down came the bed. There were no sheet or blankets but one could hire pillows for a franc from a porter who wheeled a small trolley on which rows of clean white pillows hung from a pole. The *chaufferettes* or footwarmers were changed at various stations . . .

"One had a travelling rug, but one never undressed, it was not considered safe in case of accidents. For years later, even when sleeping cars existed, I would remember Mama's warning not to undress in case of accidents and I would lie on the bed fully clothed.

"In the early hours of the morning the train stopped at Toulon and a chipped cup of coffee with a *croissant,* already moist from the overflow on the saucer, would be thrust through the window; that was all, yet one lived through it . . ."

THE FRENCH NETWORK

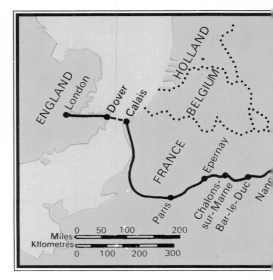

In the half-century before 1890, railway mileage in France grew at the rate of about 475 miles a year until it reached a total of 20 000 miles or so, 80 per cent of the maximum when the network was completed.

For the ordinary traveller in France – and, indeed, in the greater part of Continental Europe – a journey by rail was not an experience to look forward to. Express trains between capital cities averaged little more than 30mph; carriages were drab and uncomfortable, even for those who could afford the high fares charged for first-class travel on many routes; and second-class passengers frequently had to make do with cushionless, wooden seats.

One of the drawbacks to the improvement in speed and comfort in France was the monopoly system. In addition, the government guaranteed minimum dividends to the individual companies; the Paris, Lyons & Mediterranean, for example, had an assured return of 11 per cent, while in the case of the Northern (Nord) it was 13 per cent.

To enjoy real railway luxury you had to be able to afford not only the first-class fare but the supplement charged to travel on an international express operated by the *Compagnie Internationale des Wagons-Lits et des Grands Express Européens*.

The Orient Express

The company, founded by the Belgian, Georges Nagelmackers, had inaugurated the first of its great trains, the *Express d'Orient,* in 1883. By 1889, passengers could travel direct from Paris to Constantinople in 67 hours 35 minutes. The train was already an international legend although known to travellers and the public as the *Orient Express,* a fact which the company accepted in 1891 by abandoning the original French name.

A brief extract from an article which appeared in *Time* magazine in 1960 conveys the opulence of the most famous of all the world's trains: "The seats had velvet covers topped by Brussels lace, and lush damask curtains hung from the windows; the fittings were of solid oak and mahogany; hand-cut glass separated the sleeping compartments from the aisle.

"In elegant salon-cars, diners lingered over oysters and chilled glasses of champagne, served by attendants in morning coats, light blue silk breeches, white stockings and buckled shoes. Elegant prostitutes provided companionship for the lonely on the long journey to the Orient . . ."

Lunch in a Wagons-Lits restaurant car was sophisticated and delicious: the 'Blue Train' taking Parisians to the Riviera in 1912 (below). The romance of the 'Orient Express' (see map above) can be imagined in the luxurious surroundings (right) of the company's elegant coaches (below).

Hamlyn Group

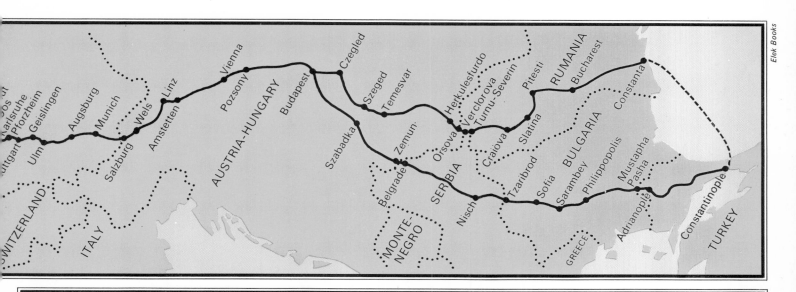

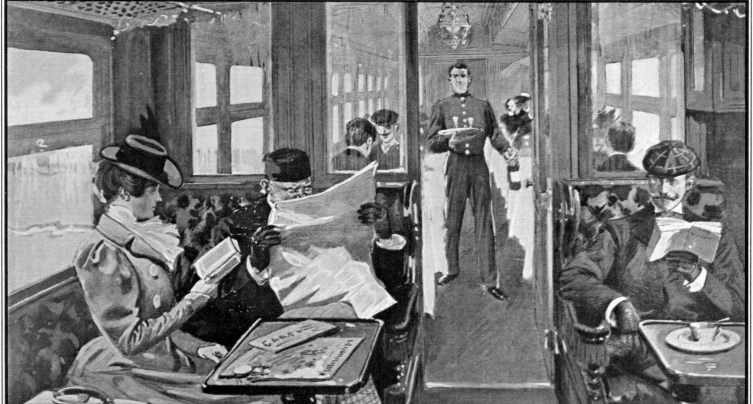

The years to the end of the century saw the inauguration of many of Europe's most famous trains. The *Calais-Nice-Rome Express* followed within a few months of the *Orient Express,* and in 1889, when its route was cut, became the *Calais-Méditerranée Express,* direct ancestor of the legendary *Blue Train.*

From 1887, Paris was linked with Madrid and Lisbon by the *Sud Express.* In 1890 came a new *Rome Express,* linking Calais with the Italian capital via the Mont Cenis tunnel and Turin. The *Ostend-Vienna Express,* designed to link London and Brussels with the *Orient Express,* started to operate in 1894.

Political pressure on the Prussians, who were hostile to *Wagons-Lits* as a foreign company, led ultimately to the successful inauguration of the *Nord Express.* The train consisted of through sleeping-cars from Ostend and Paris, which joined up at Liège, plus a dining car and wagon-restaurant-salon.

Passengers left London at 10.00 hours, and Paris at 14.15, on Saturday; arrived in Berlin at 08.43 on Sunday; reached Eydtkuhnen, eastern limit of standard gauge, at 20.40 that evening; and, after changing to Russian broad-gauge carriages, steamed into St Petersburg (now Leningrad) at 15.50 on Monday afternoon.

The popularity of the French Riviera with the titled and the famous — both Queen Victoria and her son, the Prince of Wales, were regular visitors — led in 1898 to the clumsily-titled *St Petersburg-Vienna-Nice-Cannes Express,* which began its exhausting journey at 18.00 hours every Sunday and delivered the pre-Revolution nobility in Cannes at 14.19 the following Wednesday.

Some idea of the gastronomic pleasures awaiting the traveller who put himself in the care of Nagelmackers can be gained from the following menus, served on the *Rome Express* on November 15, 1897, when, for the

La Vie du Rail

first time, the train was made up entirely of *Wagons-Lits* rolling stock. The menu for lunch was:

Hors d'Oeuvres Variés
Filets de Sole au Vin Blanc
Côtelettes de Mouton à la Mont Cenis
Petits Pois à l'Anglaise
Galantine de Volaille
Langue Écarlate
Fromage
Fruits
Café
Liqueurs

And for dinner:

Hors d'Oeuvres
Consommé à la Duchesse
Barbue, Sauce Hollandaise
Aloyau de Bœuf Rôti
Haricots Verts
Poulet de Grains
Salades
Soufflé à la Rome Express
Glaces
Fromages
Desserts
Café
Liqueurs

Railways took the French on seaside holidays; here (far left) the train arrives at Mont St Michel.
The Northern Railway of France had this giant four cylinder de Glehn-du Bousquet compound locomotive built in 1912. Known as the 'Baltic' in Europe, its boiler was fitted with a water tube firebox to improve steam production.
The Rome express (top), with Wagons-Lits coaches, leaves Paris for the South hauled by a four-cylinder compound express locomotive on the Paris, Lyons & Mediterranean Railway.

45

The basic motive behind the creation of many *Wagons-Lits* expresses was to serve the needs of the rich British traveller — eager to winter among the art treasures of Florence, to savour the increasingly sophisticated pleasures of the Riviera, or to recover from an excess of good living by taking a cure at one of Europe's celebrated spas.

The lucrative London-Paris traffic also inspired the creation of the famous de Glehn compound locomotives, 4-4-0s when they first appeared early in the 1890s, although they were followed by a 4-4-2 Atlantic type.

The compound system meant that the same steam could be used twice, first in two high-pressure cylinders, then in two low-pressure cylinders. The engines developed by Alfred de Glehn and du Bousquet, locomotive engineer of the Northern, also incorporated an ingenious method of boosting power when necessary by admitting small quantities of high-pressure steam to the low-pressure cylinders.

France leads in speed

The result was vastly improved climbing performance. In spite of the maximum speed of French trains being limited by law at this period to 120km/h (75mph), the ability of the de Glehn compounds to cope with gradients enabled the Calais-Paris run to be reduced from four and a half to three and a half hours in the course of the last decade of the century.

By 1900, in fact, the Nord was one of the fastest lines in the world and, taken overall, France led the Continent in speed, with 20 expresses running at an average of more than 56mph. Passenger comfort had not kept pace with locomotive development, however, and the traveller on French railways could rarely hope to find accommodation in anything better than a four-wheeled 'dog box'.

Even as late as the Paris Exhibition of 1900 the Orleans Railway was proud to display *new* four-wheelers which, as one British observer put it, "deserves special mention, for bad though it is, according to English notions, it nevertheless reaches a higher standard of comfort than that attained by any

other of the French companies.

"The upholstery is, of course, very slight, consisting merely of the familiar strip of hard leather on the seat, a corresponding strip at the back of each place, exactly similar to that provided in compartments of the same class on the Underground; but plenty of space is given between the seats, and the vehicle is well-lighted and roomy. The divisions between the compartments only extend for two-thirds of the height of the carriage."

Nor in the early years of the new century were French railways noted for their smooth running. The most bitter complaints came from sleeping-car passengers, who were convinced that drivers on night duty deliberately speeded up when there were tight curves or uneven points to be negotiated.

Outbreak of war

One author, who took the night sleeper from Paris to Marseilles, found the experience so shattering that he began his subsequent book of Mediterranean travels with the sentence: "The train went mad in the night."

The outbreak of war in 1914 caused severe disruption of the *Wagons-Lits* services, both across and within frontiers. German occupa-

tion of Belgium also cut the company off from its main base, which had remained in Brussels although the chief areas of *Wagons-Lits* operation were France, Italy and Russia. In 1915 it moved its headquarters to Paris where it has stayed to this day.

The railways took the rich to resorts in style. This railway poster appeared at the beginning of the century.
Alfred de Glehn (top left) was an Englishman who emigrated to Germany to become the chief designer for a French owned company in Alsace, where he evolved a compound locomotive system. The province had been ceded to Germany in 1871, but had retained its French markets, and the international influences produced, in the case of the compound express locomotive (below), the most typically French locomotive of its time. It was designed in 1905 for the Paris-Orleans Railway.
Monsieur du Bousquet (top right) was the chief engineer of the Northern Railway of France, the first French main line to use compound locomotives.

4023

Mary Evans

Wagons-Lits Co.

The demands of war imposed a crushing burden on the French railway network in general. French mobilization involved the use of 3000 trains. Moving French troops to the Western Front in the first month of the war took 400 trains and the transportation of the British Expeditionary Force to the trenches another 350.

Four hundred trains had to be organized when 52 troopships arrived at Marseilles bearing 70000 Ghurkas and Sikhs and their equipment. Repelling the persistent German attack at Verdun called for more than 3500 trains to transport 1500000 men, equipment and supplies. Seven thousand more were run as part of the back-up to the British counter-offensive on the Somme.

By mid-1916, French railways were beginning to collapse under the strain, and an appeal to Britain resulted in more than a thousand locomotives and thousands of wagons being shipped across the Channel. Little-used British rails were ripped up, sent to France and relaid.

Eventually, the British also became responsible for most of their own troop movements in France, a task handled by the Railway Operating Division of the British Army, commanded in the field by Lt.-Col. Cecil Paget, who had been general superintendent of the Midland Railway.

Paget proved a remarkable officer, disdainful of red tape, who set up mobile headquarters in a train. Each morning, he sprinted from one end to the other and back to keep fit, and then, being a *cordon bleu* chef among other things, cooked breakfast for his brother officers. His prodigies of off-the-cuff organization earned him a knighthood, and it was a tragedy for the Midland that, after the war, he made his future in industry.

In the course of the war, many *Wagons-Lits* carriages of various types were requisitioned by the military authorities for use as special trains such as ambulances, a practice that was to ensure for one of them – dining car No. 2419 – a place of distinction in the annals of both World Wars.

In October 1918, the *Wagons-Lits* company received instructions that dining car No. 2419 was to be converted into an office for Marshal Foch, the Minister of War. It was to have two rooms, with electric light, and the stove taken out to make a typist's office.

The conversion was completed at the company workshops at St Denis, on the outskirts of Paris, on October 28, and the carriage was formally requisitioned by General Weygand next day. By November 10, the dining car was at Creil, north of Paris. At 05.00 hours the following morning, the driver of a light engine was ordered to pick up the converted dining car and head for the Western Front.

At Compiègne he was directed to nearby Rethondes where he found Marshal Foch's mobile headquarters, consisting of three *Wagons-Lits* coaches – salon, diner, sleeper with a shock van at each end – and dining car No. 2419 was attached to the train.

Half an hour later, the driver and his crew were astonished to see a Compiègne engine arrive, pulling three German carriages. A number of high-ranking German officers stepped down and disappeared into the dining car. The 'war to end wars' was over: they had come to sign the Armistice.

Dining car No. 2419 subsequently had a chequered career. After Marshal Foch had used it for a number of journeys, it was presented to the French War Museum at Les Invalides where, left in the open, it deteriorated rapidly. This led to widespread criticism in French and foreign newspapers until eventually an American, Arthur Fleming, offered 150000 francs to restore the carriage and find it a home under cover at Compiègne.

The offer was accepted. Dining car No. 2419, restored by the *Wagons-Lits* company works at St Denis, housed indoors and cared for by a former sergeant in the French Army, became a popular tourist attraction. On June 20, 1940, however, the Germans entered Rethondes, dragged the dining car into the open and placed it on the exact spot where, more than 20 years earlier, the Armistice had been signed.

There, two days later, Hitler dictated the terms of French surrender before ordering that the carriage should be brought to Berlin and that the rails on which it had rested for both Armistice negotiations were to be destroyed "so that no trace of the 1918 German defeat should remain."

After being transported to the German capital by road, dining car No. 2419, with the original of the Treaty of Versailles displayed inside it, was visited by large crowds. By the end of the war it had found its way to Ohr-druf, a small town in central Germany, where it was blown up by a special detachment of SS men as American tanks approached.

Since 1950, another *Wagons-Lits* dining car of a slightly different type has taken the place of No. 2419 at Rethondes.

The *Orient Express,* most distinguished casualty of the First World War, did not start to run again until some time after the end of hostilities. Instead, its function was fulfilled by a new express, the *Simplon-Orient,* destined to be as famous as its precursor.

The Simplon tunnel, longest (12.33 miles) in the world and offering a more direct route to Milan, had been opened in 1906 with electric locomotives hauling passenger trains from the outset, and *Wagons-Lits* had immediately inaugurated the *Simplon Express* (Paris, Lausanne, Brig, Simplon, Milan).

The destination of the express was extended to Venice in 1907 and to Trieste in 1912. With the war over and the Allies, at this stage, eager to maintain east-west communications without traversing German or Austrian territory, the logical development was to create the *Simplon-Orient,* extending the route again from Trieste to Belgrade and Bucharest, then on from Belgrade to Istanbul.

Wagons-Lits were made responsible for running the train, which was inaugurated on April 11, 1919. The express itself was, however, the creation of politicians rather than railwaymen. With hindsight, it is possible to look upon this as an omen of what lay ahead for the railways of the world.

Fares before 1914 were twice today's in real terms, which made single-coach passenger trains economic. Top left: The coach for Venice leaves Calais in 1908, hauled by a de Glehn-du Bousquet compound Atlantic type locomotive, designed in 1900.
The Wagons-Lits restaurant car No. 2419 was used to sign armistices in both World Wars. Left: Marshall Foch is prominent at the signing in Rethonde. Above: Hitler, followed by Göring comes to sign the peace between Germany and France in 1940.
The Brig exit of the Simplon tunnel, first opened in 1906 (left).

RAILWAYS UNITE

Initially, the railway was seen in Germany as a means of enabling horses to haul heavier loads. As early as 1815, Josef Ritter von Baader, a Bavarian mining expert who had worked for many years in Britain, was granted the first German railway patent, to build a track for the transportation of goods between Nuremberg and the neighbouring town of Fürth. Although von Baader was familiar with the work of Trevithick, he designed the power to be provided by horses.

It was to be 20 years before the line was actually built, however. The man behind it then was not von Baader but a citizen of Nuremberg, Johannes Scharrer, and the concept was entirely different. The trains were to be hauled by locomotives and, in the light of English experience, provision was to be made for passengers as well as goods traffic.

Work began once King Ludwig of Bavaria had given his assent in February 1834. To avoid prohibitive customs duties, one 10-ft rail was imported from England and copied locally. Wagons and carriages were also built in Germany, but the railway company took the precaution of ordering a *Patentee*-type locomotive, complete with driver, from Robert Stephenson & Company.

Amid mounting excitement, the locomotive had already been named *Der Adler* (The Eagle) when it arrived in parts with its accompanying driver, Mr Wilson, who was considered such an important figure that he was paid more than the head of the company.

The line, called the *Ludwigsbahn* in honour of the king, opened towards the end of 1835 and was a huge success from the start, with passengers buying more than 1200 tickets a day. Wilson, who had originally planned to stay just a few months, changed his mind under the influences of his generous salary and the prestige of being Germany's first engine-driver. He learned German, settled down for 27 years and became a much-admired local celebrity.

Until shortly before this time, Germany had been a loose federation of separate states, each jealous of its own sovereignty. Anyone

The first railway in Germany was opened in 1835 (right) and ran from Nuremberg to Fürth. The locomotive was Robert Stephenson's 'Patentee'-type 'Der Adler', which was imported from Britain complete with William Wilson, the driver.

GERMANY

The Würtemberg State Railway was opened in 1845. The first engines were imported from the United States and locomotive builders tended to copy these designs. Gradually the American features were absorbed into European practice. The 'Berg' (below) was designed in 1856 but not built until 1860, when the absorption process was under way.

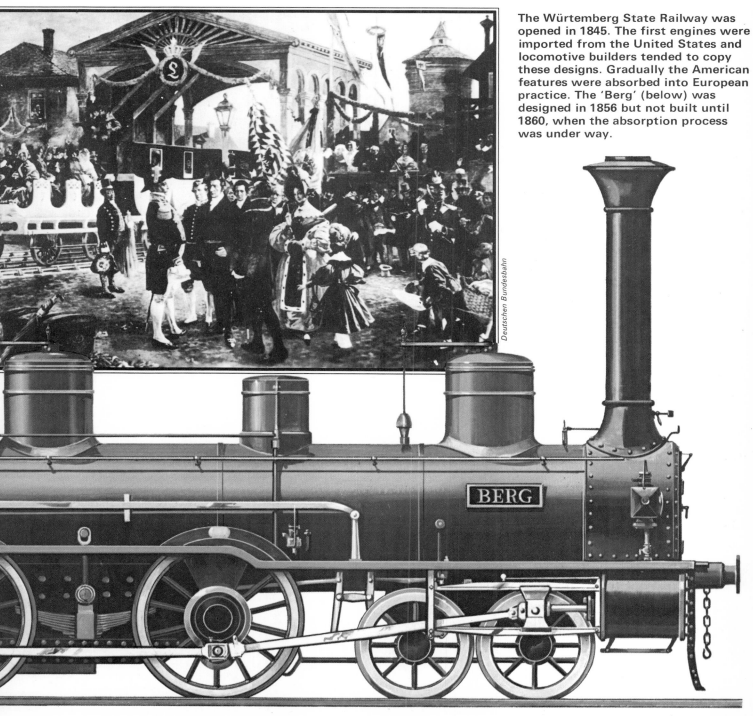

Deutschen Bundesbahn

BERG

Deutschen Bundesbahn

travelling from the North Sea to the Alps had to cross – and pay customs duty to – what were in practical effect ten countries with a variety of currencies. Their population was made up largely of peasants who faced famine in years of bad harvests.

One of the voices arguing in favour of unity, and development of the railway, as an answer to the country's economic plight was Friedrich List, Professor of Economics at Tübingen. He was promptly jailed for meddling in political affairs that were none of his business. By 1834, however, the climate had changed and this year saw the formation of the German Customs Union, the first step in the direction of economic, and ultimately political, union.

Railway fever

The country was now swept by the same kind of railway fever which had gripped Britain a decade earlier after the success of the Stockton-Darlington line. Railway companies sprang up everywhere. A section of a line planned from Dresden to Leipzig was opened in 1837. The next year saw the opening of Prussia's first railway, from Potsdam to Berlin-Zehlendorf.

The Rhenish Railway completed its line from Cologne to Aachen in 1841, and, two years later, to Herbesthal where the track linked up with the Belgian State Railway. The Belgian State, which was the world's first planned national railway system, had been built to provide trade routes which the hostile Netherlands could not interfere with, since Belgium had recently obtained independence. The ceremonial laying of the link rail at Herbesthal on October 15, 1843 was an important event in railway history, the first time two independent nations with different languages and different traditions had been joined by the iron way.

In many parts of the country peasants opposed the coming of the railway just as bitterly as the rich landowners had done in England. The Prussian Railway Act of 1838 gave railways the right to expropriate the land they needed and provided for some supervision of the predominantly-private companies. The state had control over routes, rolling stock and locomotives, and safety standards. Permanent officials were appointed to supervise the finances of the companies.

The Act also gave the state the right to buy the companies out after 30 years.

By 1845, Germany had 1900 miles of track, more than half of it in Prussia, and the total nearly doubled in the next five years. The great 'wheel' of the German railway system – with Berlin as the axle and spokes radiating to Danzig in the east, Cologne in the west, Hamburg to the north and Munich to the south – had begun to take shape.

The tense political climate of Europe at the time also saw the state take an increasing part in financing railway development for strategic rather than economic reasons. The ability of trains to move large numbers of men and large quantities of guns and materials to a crisis area in a short time was not lost on the military mind.

German railways reached out to the French frontier in 1852, to the Dutch in 1856. From the following year it was possible to take a through coach from Frankfurt to Basle in Switzerland, and, in 1860, a standard-gauge Prussian line linked up with the broad gauge of Russia at Eydtkuhnen. The possible advantages to an enemy of a line on the west bank of the Rhine also led to Prussia blocking its construction for many years.

Inspired plan

The link at Eydtkuhnen was to inspire Georges Nagelmackers, founder of the *Compagnie Internationale des Wagons-Lits et des Grands Express Européens*, to an imaginative plan 23 years later which was to defeat even his formidable powers of persuasion and organization.

In 1883, soon after the start of the *Orient Express*, he began working out details of a *Nord-Sud Express* which would connect St Petersburg (now Leningrad) with Lisbon via Eydtkuhnen, Berlin, Cologne, Herbesthal, Liège, Erquelines, Paris, Irún, Madrid and Valencia de Alcántara.

In April 1884, Nagelmackers actually published a tentative timetable for the proposed journey of 3021 miles (4834 kilometres), which involved changes from broad gauge to standard when the coaches left Russia and back to broad gauge when they entered Spain. The train would leave St Petersburg on the evening of Day One, arrive in Berlin at 23.50 on Day Two, reach Paris at 16.32 on Day Three, arrive in Madrid at 20.18 on Day

Mary Evans

William Wilson (far left) came from England to Germany to drive the first German railway train in 1835, on a salary higher than anyone else in the company. He was in charge of locomotives in Germany until his death 27 years later. The Saxon State Railway was opened in 1837 with a line running from Dresden to Leipzig. The first train on this railway (left) took carriages without horses, the passengers sitting in the open, 'guarded' by the coachman.
The locomotive works in Esslingen produced the 'Kopernicus' in 1858. Emil Kessler took photographs of most of the locomotives his plant produced, often with the church spire in the background, as seen here (below).

Deutschen Bundesbahn

Four and be in Lisbon at 10.25 the following morning.

One section of the train was to be detached at Liège to connect with London via Calais. To overcome the gauge problem, Nagelmackers proposed to use coaches with special bogies which would take axles and wheels of three different gauges. He had allowed 25 minutes for axle-changing at the Russian frontier, 35 at the Spanish.

This daunting scheme foundered largely on Prussian opposition to *Wagons-Lits* as a foreign company making money out of Germany. Several of the internal services which Nagelmackers had contracted for, including Eydtkuhnen-Berlin and Berlin-Cologne, were suspended in the 1880s, and the Prussian and Hessian Railways operated their own sleeping cars.

Homemade

To avoid customs duties, Germany had rolled its own rails for the Nuremberg-Fürth line, and, as a major industrial country, it built its own locomotives. By 1863, only 520 of the 3860 locomotives running in the country, — less than 15 per cent — were of foreign origin, and the names of Borsig, Henschel and Maffei were eventually as highly-rated as that of Robert Stephenson & Company. Indeed, Henschel Lokomotiven and Krauss-Maffei still build today's electric and diesel locomotives.

The search for a satisfactory brake that would bring a whole train to a stop led to the development in Germany in 1847 of the Exter brake, a system of cords and pulleys which allowed up to four following carriages or wagons to be braked from a handwheel in

RTHPL

Climbing steep gradients was a problem overcome by introducing the cog wheel on the locomotive, which engaged with a rack laid between the rails. The Kahlenberg rack railway (above) was opened in 1874, and climbed the steep gradients past Grinzing to the beautiful Vienna woods. A route from Vienna to Cracow was jointly undertaken by Robert Stephenson and a Venetian, Carlo di Ghega (top right). In the 1850s Ghega planned and built the Semmering railway across the Austrian Alps. On express locomotives a lightly loaded pair of wheels was usually fitted ahead of the driving wheels; below, however, an 1872 locomotive from Carl Ludwig's Railway has the driving wheels placed in front.

the locomotive tender. George Westinghouse, who devised the continuous air brake in 1869 when he was only 23, was an American inventor of German extraction. It was also the German firm of Krupp which, in 1850, produced the first steel locomotive tire and the first steel locomotive axles.

Steel tires

This was an important advance on the wrought iron which had been used previously. Wrought iron tires were a source of trouble because they did not wear well and tended to be squeezed out of shape by the weight of the locomotive as it ran on the rails. Steel was a great improvement and, although expensive, steel tires soon came into general use in Germany and France, and were even exported to Britain.

The forging and treatment of steel was not fully understood at this time, however, and both tires and axles showed a tendency to break unexpectedly. It was the British inventor, Henry Bessemer, who finally overcame this failing when he developed his steel converter in 1856. Within a couple of years, large quantities of high-quality steel became available at low cost and the Iron Age of the railways was over.

Although rail travel throughout Germany, and eventually to east and west, became an increasing reality throughout the first quarter of a century of railway development, the great barrier to the south – the Alps, stretching from Nice in the south of France to Vienna – had still not been pierced. The traveller between Germany and Italy had to abandon his modern train and resort to stagecoach to cross the mountains.

This is not to say that railways were unknown in the Alpine countries of Switzerland and Austria. Switzerland was linked with France (Strasbourg-Basle) in 1841 and had its first internal railway, the Zürich-Baden, in 1847. The second of these lines was popularly known as the 'Spanish Bun Railway' because it carried supplies of *Spanischen Brötli*, a Baden speciality, to Zürich breakfast tables.

Austria, for its part, was not far behind Germany in entering the Railway Age. Its first public steam railway, the *Kaiser Ferdinand Nordbahn*, ran between Vienna, Floridsdorf and Wagram from 1837. The Vienna-Gloggnitz line to the south-west opened in 1841, offering early locomotives the challenge of gradients of 1:200. But at Gloggnitz the towering mountains brought Austrian railway development to a halt.

Alpine challenge

The man who decided to challenge the Alps was a Venetian engineer, Carlo di Ghega, who refused to accept George Stephenson's view that it was 'impossible' to build a line over the mountainous section between Gloggnitz and Mürzzuschlag – the Semmering Pass – to connect with Graz, Laibach (now in Yugoslavia and called Ljubljana) and Trieste on the Adriatic. He began by visiting the United States where, after extensive study of railroad operations over difficult terrain, he came to the conclusion that a gradient of 1:30 was not beyond a locomotive of the right type on the right kind of track.

The line – Europe's first planned mountain railway – was begun in 1846, with government backing, and took 11 years to complete

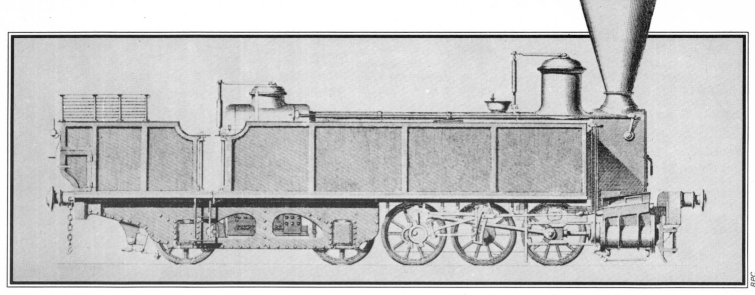
BPC

to Trieste, a hundred miles beyond the mountains. Tunnels and galleries were carved out of solid rock, bridges built across ravines, using gunpowder, hand drills and horses for haulage, and, by the time the task was finished, 700 men had given their lives, struck down by cholera and typhus.

While the work went ahead, doubts were still being expressed about whether a locomotive would be able to cope with the gradients. A competition rather like the one which produced Stephenson's *Rocket* was therefore run in 1851 with a first prize of 20 000 ducats.

There were four entries, the *Bavaria* by Maffei of Munich, the *Seraing* from Belgium, and two Austrian locomotives, the *Wiener-Neustadt* and the *Vindobona*. The task set them was to haul a load of 140 tons at a speed of at least seven mph up a gradient of 1:40. All four succeeded, although sanding of the rails was forbidden.

Iron horse or mountain goat

Even the *Bavaria,* which was awarded first prize, revealed certain deficiencies, however, and the Professor of Engineering at Graz was commissioned to design a fifth locomotive, classified as 'a Semmering Locomotive, Engerth System'. On April 12, 1854, it hauled the first train over the Semmering Pass, trundling uphill at 11mph and downhill at the same speed with brakes on. In the face of all the doubts, di Ghega had proved that the 'iron horse' could be a mountain creature.

The Brenner Pass, with a line reaching a height of 4496 feet above sea level, opened up the route between Innsbruck and Bolzano in 1867. It was followed by the Mont Cenis (Fréjus) tunnel between France and Lombardy in 1871, and in 1872 work began on the nine and a half-mile St Gotthard tunnel, a joint German-Swiss-Italian project in the interests of greater trade.

Its engineer was Louis Favre, already celebrated for his tunnel-building in France. The monumental task involved the construction of 324 bridges and viaducts. Apart from the summit tunnel itself, Favre eased the gradient by cutting 28 miles of single and double climbing spirals over viaducts and through the hearts of mountains. On February 29, 1880, the last section of rock fell and the moment of triumph was celebrated by carry-

The Semmering competition in 1851 was won by Wilhelm Engerth. In the original design, gear wheels from the rear driving wheels drove the articulated tender; the gears were later abandoned to produce this modified Engerth engine (above). Another entry was the 'Bavaria' (above right). Its three sets of driving wheels were connected by sprockets and chains, but the chains proved unsatisfactory. The Alps presented a tremendous challenge to engineers. The Swiss entrance to the St Gotthard tunnel (right); and (top right) the workmen from either end meet underground on February 29, 1880.

ing a picture of Favre through the gap. He himself had died a year earlier while supervising work on his masterpiece.

The last of the famous Alpine tunnels to be completed before 1890 was the 1100-yard Arlberg, linking Zürich and the west of Austria with the line to Innsbruck and the east, which opened in 1884. It emerged on the eastern side at a tiny hamlet named St Anton. Today, as the train appears out of the darkness, the first vision for passengers are the slopes of what has become one of the world's most famous ski resorts.

Politically, railways in Germany – with a history of cooperation in such practical matters as fares, plus the opportunities they offered for travel – proved an important influence in bringing about the eventual unification of the country. As the historian Heinrich von Treitschke put it: "The frontiers of the races and the states lost their disruptive power, rivalries were forgotten and the Germans discovered the pleasure of getting to know one another."

Bismarck dreamed of a single German railway to serve the unified German nation. This was not a popular idea initially with many of the individual state systems. The period 1870 to 1890, however, did see most of the private lines taken over. In these 20 years, lines under private ownership decreased from 5000 miles to 2000, while those controlled by the states doubled from 12 000 to 24 000. It was the start of an evolutionary process which led eventually to the formation of the *Reichsbahn* in 1924.

GERMANY LINKS

Railways came comparatively slowly to Germany, made up in the mid-nineteenth century of individual states with largely rural populations and strong conservative traditions. A comparison with the mileage of track in Britain is revealing, particularly considering the much greater area of Germany:

	1850	1860	1870	1887	1903
Britain	6620	10430	15540	19810	22152
Germany	3640	6980	11730	24270	32477

It was not that Germany did not need railways. The growth of the Industrial Revolution produced the same social effects as it had in Britain — a gradual drift from the land, growth of the towns and cities, and the development of a mass market for cheap goods. Berlin, for instance, which had barely 300 000 inhabitants in 1845, could claim a population of around one and a half million by 1890.

The independence of the states, however, was an impediment to creating a complete and unified system of internal transport, so vital for industrial prosperity, until Bismarck succeeded in uniting the country in 1871.

In the next 17 years, track mileage more than doubled and the British total was surpassed. The spirit of independence was still strong, however, and Bismarck's attempts to unify German railroads under the administration of the imperial government failed in the face of opposition from the larger states. Once this battle had been won, Prussia proceeded to nationalize her lines, an example followed by all the other states until, by 1904, only 2807 miles of standard-gauge track remained in private hands.

The states cooperate

Despite reluctance to lose their own identity, the individual states showed themselves willing to use their railroads to further broad German interests. Prussia, for example, largest of the state systems, brought in cheap freight rates on raw materials for ship construction when there was a movement to extend German shipbuilding.

Prussia also cooperated with Hamburg steamship companies to offer a very low rail-sea freight rate from inland industrial centres to ports in the Levant and East Africa, thus persuading German shippers to use German ships rather than those of other countries.

Railway profits became an increasingly important element in the income of the various states, averaging around 40 per cent by the early years of this century, and, governments being what they are, they had no difficulty in finding ways of spending the money.

It need hardly be said that low priority was given, if any priority was given at all, to improving the lot of the travellers who had helped to provide the money in the first place. Despite recurrent protests, Prussia even retained its fourth-class passenger service, for which the word 'spartan' seems, in retrospect, flattering. Passengers travelled in bare, four-wheeled 'dog-boxes' with a few seats around the walls. Sixty was a normal load, and anyone who did not bring a stool with them usually had to stand.

German trains were also appallingly slow as the century entered its last decade. Professor Foxwell and Lord Farrer had harsh things to say about them in their famous statistical analysis of the world's expresses of the period:

"The Bavarian, Würtemberg and Saxon railways are a disgrace to Europe as far as speed goes. It is positively two hours quicker

EUROPE

to go from London to Vienna all the way round Paris (100 miles further) owing to the slowness of the trains in Bavaria and Würtemberg.

"The governments of these countries have always owned their railways and worked them, and we have a good illustration of the sort of effeteness that state management produces after a time. There is practically no fast third-class accommodation in Bavaria or Würtemberg. The *Orient Express* runs faster in Rumania than in Würtemberg . . .''

Chaos at Basle

The one exception to these strictures was the 'crack' southbound express of the Baden State Railway which, on the 162-mile run between Mannheim and the Swiss frontier city of Basle, averaged 34mph, including stops totalling around half an hour at seven stations. This was a highly respectable performance by the standards of the era.

It was just as well to arrive fresh and relaxed at Basle which, despite its international importance, was renowned at this time as a place of chaos guaranteed to turn the sensitive traveller into a wreck.

To be there early in the morning was to see Basle at its worst. Between 05.30 and 06.34 hours, seven international expresses arrived from Paris, Ostend, Berlin, Boulogne, Frankfurt and Cologne, were remarshalled, and between 06.50 and 07.40 departed again for Lucerne or for Milan, via the St Gotthard.

Although Basle had six through lines, the passengers from all these trains were dealt with at a single platform, which became for these two hours a seething mass of multi-lingual humanity, stampeding to and fro in search of something to eat, something to drink, a wash, information, porters or vanished luggage.

If they strayed to one end of the platform, they were rounded up by German police or pounced upon by German customs officials: if they strayed to the other they were rounded up by Swiss police or pounced upon by Swiss customs officials. To fight your way into a waiting room was an achievement to be talked about with pride; to extricate yourself once you were inside was an even greater achievement.

The frenzy on the platform was mirrored on the tracks. Scores of railwaymen with hand signals shouted, cursed and tooted horns as they struggled to sort out six-wheelers and bogie coaches belonging to a variety of owners — Swiss railways, French railways, German railways, the Gotthard Railway and *Wagons-Lits*. Their task was not made any easier by the existence, at the German end of the station, of a level crossing which had to be opened and closed throughout the shunting operations to allow street traffic to pass.

Between 1900 and 1914, a number of improvements were made in the arrangements for handling rolling stock and passengers, but it was not until well after the First World War that Basle achieved anything like the degree of sophistication one expects in a station of such international importance.

The Royal Prussian Union Railway's Class S²10 built from 1914 onwards, was the line's crack express. The design used three simple expansion cylinders instead of the earlier Class S'10's four cylinder compound system. The rough conditions of RPUR's fourth class are seen through a sentimental eye in Eugen Urban's study (above).

Over the years, Germany contributed important improvements to the steam locomotive as well as to the electric and diesel locomotives which would one day largely replace them.

The German engineer Werner von Siemens demonstrated his first successful DC electric motor as early as 1879, although the switch to this form of traction did not really gather pace until the inter-war years.

Similarly, Rudolf Diesel demonstrated a diesel motor in 1897. But early diesel locomotives proved unsatisfactory because of recurrent transmission failure and their day did not come until a means had been found of turning diesel power into electricity and using the electricity to drive the wheels, first accomplished in Sweden in 1912.

Germany's two most memorable contributions to the steam era were the superheating process, developed by Dr Wilhelm Schmidt, a consultant to the Prussian State Railways, and the work of the Maffei company in Bavaria on compound locomotives.

If steam is superheated, it expands and its capacity for work increases. This principle, with its twin advantages of greater efficiency and lower coal consumption, was adopted with enthusiasm by Prussia for its locomotives, followed by railway systems in the other German states, Austria, Belgium, France, Sweden, Switzerland, and even by countries as far away as Canada and South Africa.

Until the middle of the first decade of this century, nearly all compound locomotives had followed the practice of Alfred de Glehn, the famous British designer who worked in France, with two cylinders driving the leading pair of coupled wheels and the other two cylinders driving the rear pair.

Maffei's departure was to set all four cylinders in line and apply the drive solely to the front axle. The resulting 4-6-0 design did not receive universal acceptance — many railway engineers took the view that it was an error to have all the stresses on one axle, and this, in addition, could cause damage to the permanent way — but Maffei had produced a well-balanced locomotive which combined power with economy well ahead of its time.

The St Gotthard tunnel

In 1907, compounds developed from the Maffei design took over from de Glehns's on the difficult St Gotthard tunnel route, which inflicted on passengers a slow and stifling journey as they sat in airless compartments with all the windows shut to keep out the smoke and soot.

As Richard Bagot wrote in 1905: "To those fresh from a journey from Basle through the St Gotthard Pass, the change from a stuffy railway carriage — very likely shared in the company of a German couple on their *voyage de noces*, who have devoted themselves to amorous triflings, embarrassing enough to any but Teutonic spectators — to the little steamer which conveys travellers from Lugano to Porlezza and Italy is grateful enough".

Dr Rudolph Diesel (top) whose name is now given to the oil engine; left is a German design of 1893. Before Diesel's work, Ackroyd Stuart in England had been producing oil engines, and in 1894 a unit powered the world's first diesel locomotive at trials in Hull.
Wilhelm Schmidt (right) invented the steam superheater, which was first used in 1898 on a German locomotive; the definitive design was used in 1903 on a Belgian locomotive.
The Royal Prussian Union Railway's Class G8¹ (below) is the third most numerous class in the world. Between 1913 and 1933 5297 were built and used in over 20 countries in three continents.

La Vie du Rail

The introduction of the more powerful German locomotives did not render this complaint obsolete. It took two of them to haul most trains while even the fastest international expresses were allowed 49 minutes to negotiate the 21 tunnels, continuous curves and 1:38/39 gradient over the 18 miles of track between Erstfeld and Göschenen, northern entrance to the St Gotthard. Modern electric locomotives sail up this approach in half the time.

By the outbreak of the First World War, German main lines had shown a dramatic improvement, both in speed and passenger comforts. J. P. Pearson, the London clerk who spent nearly all his spare time either travelling in trains or writing about journeys he had made in trains, had only praise for the trip he made between Hamburg and Berlin in the summer of 1913:

Railways for war

". . . one of my finest runs up till now on the Continent . . . Our engine on this splendid run was an *Altona division* 4-6-0 (No. 1102) and, for a very short distance out of Hamburg, a pusher behind gave us a good send-off with our enormous load (for 1913) of 438 tons empty (I can hardly estimate what the weight 'with passengers' would be, as our 11 heavy eight-wheelers were packed, and people were standing in the corridors as well.)

" . . . the book speed of this train throughout its journey was nearly 54mph and was slightly improved on! . . . Our train crowd was well looked after at this holiday season, as not only were coffee and beef tea brought round by means of the corridor, but also beer, port and sherry."

The lesson that trains could move vast armies over large distances in a comparatively short time had been well absorbed during the Franco-Prussian war, and, in the intervening 43 years, strategic considerations had influenced much of the new track-laying in France and Germany, not to mention the creation of specialized units which could build railways, operate them, and, if necessary, blow them up.

Between the end of the Franco-Prussian war and 1913, France increased the number

of lines running east, towards the common frontier with Germany, from three to ten. Germany took similar steps. By 1911, bridges carried German rails over the Rhine at 19 points, nearly all of them double-track lines running to the west or north-east. Fourteen lines provided connecting routes with Belgium, Holland and Luxembourg. The Belgians also helped with an extension of the German Weismes-Malmédy light railway four miles across the frontier to Stavelot in Belgium, which opened up a fresh way to Liège and Brussels.

Ten months after this line was opened, it was used for the invasion by Germany. As Ernest Carter points out in his valuable book *Railways in Wartime:* "Truly it has been said that in the construction of this short piece of line, the Belgians dug their own grave, for so well was this 'light railway' built that trains could use it at speeds of up to 40mph instead of the recognized light railways speed of a maximum 16mph." On the other hand if matters had fallen out that way it would have been useful for armies invading Germany.

The war wiped out all *Wagons-Lits* services in Germany and nearly all of them in Austria. The gap was filled by *Mitropa* — the *Mitteleuropäische Schlaf und Speisewagen Gesellschaft* — using requisitioned *Wagons-Lits* rolling stock. In a postcard of the time, showing exterior and interior views of a *Mitropa* diner, the initials 'WL' are clearly visible, embossed on the back of the leather chairs.

The locomotive (top left) was built in 1909 for the RPUR's first electric line. In trials the experimental motor coach (top right) reached 130mph in 1903, but electric current had to be collected from three different sources. At a more leisurely pace the Cologne express is guided through the streets of Hamburg with a red flag to warn the inhabitants (below left).
A typical wartime scene as troops leave for the front in 1914 (left).
The 'Simplon-Orient' express curves round the lake by a Swiss chateau.

By 1917, *Wagons-Lits* had only two diners and one sleeper still operating in Austria. The trains of which they formed part were regularly hauled by one of the imaginative locomotives designed by Karl Gölsdorf. Gölsdorf, son of the senior mechanical engineer of the Austrian Southern Railway, was appointed to a similar position with the Imperial Royal Austrian State Railways in 1893 when only 32-years old, and in the next 20 years he produced no fewer than 46 new locomotive designs.

One of the great difficulties about compounding in its early stages was that maximum efficiency, particularly when starting to move, involved complex controls that were beyond the skills of most engine drivers. Gölsdorf's first memorable achievement was to invent a version of automatic control.

The locomotives he was producing at this

time were strictly functional. However, after a visit to Britain in 1899, where he was impressed by the uncluttered elegance of British designs, he became increasingly interested in appearance and eventually produced locomotives that combined style and power to a degree matched by no other continental railway system.

Gölsdorf's engines

In his book *Continental Main Lines,* the engineer and writer Oswald Nock has an affectionate description of the massive 2-10-0s built by Gölsdorf in 1906 for the Arlberg tunnel route, whose forbidding gradients and curves make it one of the most severe in Europe:

"Quite apart from their great size it was also the striking finish and the immaculate condition in which they were kept that attracted attention to these engines. The frames, wheels, cabs and tenders were black, plentifully adorned with polished brasswork, but the boilers and fireboxes were a light steel blue, lined out in black and white.

"The domes were of polished brass and round the neck of the chimney there was a copper band, to indicate that the locomotive was fitted with Gölsdorf's smoke-consuming apparatus . . ."

Gölsdorf died in 1916 at the early age of 55. Whether he would have added substantially to his earlier achievements had he lived to see the peace is debatable. The post-war break-up of its empire left Austria with only one main line – Vienna-Innsbruck-Arlberg – and that was soon electrified.

In Germany, too, there were dramatic changes. The Allies ran German railways as a single unit in the immediate aftermath of the war and urged the retention of centralized control when the time came to hand them back. Bismarck's ambition of half a century earlier finally became reality in 1920 when the *Reichsbahn* was formed and the individual state railways disappeared.

Karl Gölsdorf (1861–1916) was the chief mechanical engineer of the Austrian State Railway for over 20 years.
Good food, wine and company seem to have passed the time on the long journey from St Petersburg, through Austria to Nice on the French Riviera. This scene was painted in about 1910. The famous suspension monorail line at Elberfeld opened to traffic in 1901. It is still running successfully today.

Mary Evans

THE MOBILIZATION O

Scala

60

ITALY

The first railway in Italy, which opened on October 4, 1839, using Stephenson's *Patentee* locomotives, ran between Naples and Portici and was born largely of military considerations. The five miles of track linked the residence of Ferdinand II, King of the Two Sicilies, with his troops' barracks and arsenals. The king evidently had doubts about this new means of transport for, on the opening day, the first train conveyed government employees and soldiers. It was only when these experimental passengers had arrived back safely at Naples from Portici that the king and state dignitaries embarked on their first railway journey.

In Italy, as in Germany, the political situation was a barrier to rapid development of the railways. The country was divided into a number of kingdoms and duchies while Austria ruled the greater part of the Po valley in the north. The multiplicity of frontiers, and the fears of the individual states — quite correct, as it turned out — that ease of communications would contribute to loss of their sovereignty, encouraged caution; so that Italy, although ranking seventh in the world in terms of railway mileage, had only 269.5 miles of track in 1850 (plus the 109 miles in the Po Valley, then ruled by Austria).

The Milan-Monza line, in territory then under Austrian control, had opened in 1840. It was followed two years later by the line linking Padua with Mestre and, by boat across the lagoon, with Venice. The Pisa-Leghorn route, with Florence as its ultimate goal, was completed in 1844, and the Turin-Moncalieri line also in the north, was finished in 1848. Largely because of opposition from the chair of St Peter, the Papal States had to wait until 1856 for their first railway when Pope Pius IX had a line built between Rome and Frascati for the benefit of pilgrims. Three years later, the railway presented him with a special saloon coach.

The first railway in Italy was the Naples to Portici line, which was opened in 1839. Fergola recorded the inauguration (opposite). The Upper Italy Railway design office in Turin produced many fine locomotives from 1872 onwards; among them was 'Cleopatra' (below), built in 1878.
Passengers at Frascati had to climb steps at Frascati station to surmount a gradient that the railway couldn't negotiate. The old station (above) was opened in 1856 as a terminus of a line from Rome. By 1884 a different route brought the railway nearer to the city, now a Roman suburb.

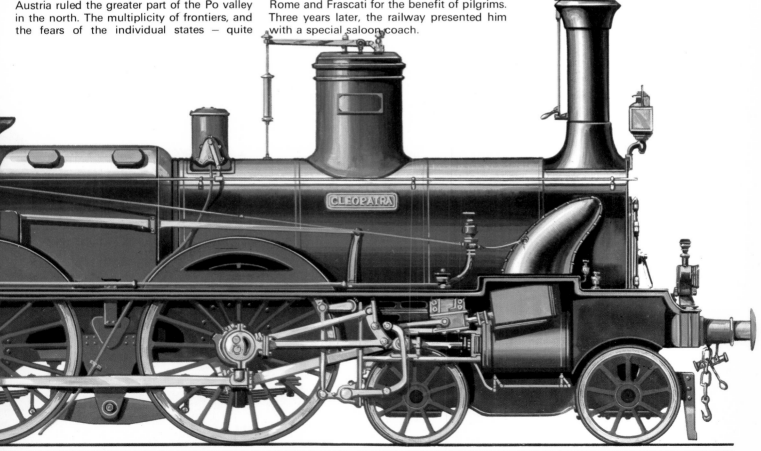

By then, particularly in Piedmont, railways had begun to spread rapidly. Piedmont, the most important state, was ruled by King Victor Emmanuel and his minister Cavour who was dedicated to the unification of Italy. Cavour had grasped the importance of the railway in the achievement of his ambition and as a means of moving troops swiftly to counter Austrian threats. With the aid of British capital and the ubiquitous British contractor Brassey, Cavour pushed development of the railway ahead, including the link with Savoy — King Victor Emmanuel was also Duke of Savoy. This involved construction of the first great Alpine tunnel, the Mont Cenis.

Cavour believed that the troops of his French ally, Napoleon II, would prove decisive in the event of war with Austria. This hope was not exactly realized when hostilities finally broke out in 1859, but, nevertheless, the war ended in 1861 with defeat for Austria, largely because of the speed with which the railways made it possible for Cavour to mobilize his own forces. The united Italy which emerged as a result of this victory had 1335 miles of railway track in use, another 1208 under construction and a further 834 in the planning stage.

Government aid

In the interests of the unity of the nation, the new government encouraged railway development as much as possible. Its main instrument was an offer to reimburse private companies for a substantial part of their construction costs once a line was open. The next few years consequently saw several important events in the history of Italian rail travel. The Naples-Rome line was completed in 1863; Florence was linked with the Milan-Venice main line in 1864; and the Rome-Florence line was opened in 1866. A year later an international route was completed from Verona to Bolzano and over the Brenner Pass to Innsbruck in Austria.

A multiplicity of companies was involved in these developments, and, in many cases, their main concern was, to get the line operating and their hands on the government subsidy. As P. M. Kalla-Bishop points out in his book *Mediterranean Island Railways*, this led to a skimping of the soundest construction principles and: "Even today the Italian State

Railways is still making good the errors of 100 years ago, straightening curves and relocating railways to cut the cost of operation and maintenance."

In an attempt to place the railroad companies on a sounder financial footing, and to secure more efficient operation, the government placed the railways under the control of three companies from 1865. The Upper Italy Railways ran the northern routes; the Roman Railroads was responsible for the Florence-Rome-Naples line and the central routes; and the Calabrian-Sicilian Railroads operated south of Naples. In addition, a fourth company, the Southern Railroads *(Strade Ferrate Meridionali)* was created to open a new route down the Adriatic coast and, in the course of the 1860s, completed a line from Bologna in the north to Lecce in the heel of Italy.

Neapolitan navvies

Brassey played an important part in the development of the railway in many parts of the country, bringing his English engineers with him but relying on local labour. As Terry Coleman records in his book *The Railway Navvies*: "On one line the Neapolitans came in large troops under their chieftains. Each chief would take perhaps 10 miles of earthworks and cuttings . . . They left their women behind, but brought their old men and boys, and built huts of wood, which they left in charge of the old men, who also cooked the food . . . Those who came to work on the line south of Naples . . . ate only bread and vegetables and drank water and goat's milk. After six months they would take their money and return to the mountains . . ."

However, in the course of the years Italy also produced her own great railway contractors. One was Count Giacomo Ceconi (1833–1910), a nearly illiterate peasant from north-east Italy, but blessed with great organizing ability. In the 1870s he built many of the works and tunnels on the Udine-Pontebba route, which formed another link between Italy and Austria when it was completed in 1879.

In the 1880s he worked on the Arlberg line, leading from the Swiss border at Buchs through western Austria to Innsbruck. The Austrian emperor, Franz Josef I, ennobled him in 1885 for his work in building the

To connect Venice to the mainland a
railway viaduct had to cross the lagoon.
It took four years to build and the 222
arches carried trains for 2¾ miles. It
was opened (left) in 1846.

The railway lines on either side of the
river Tiber in Rome were linked by the
Ostia Bridge, which was prefabricated
in Britain. Pope Pius IX made an
official visit in 1857 to observe its
construction (below), although it was
not formally opened until 1863.

In Florence the Porta al Prato station
was opened in 1848. Some idea of its
magnificence can be seen in the
elaborate station interior (right). It has
recently been incorporated into the
Florence locomotive works as a store
and warehouse.

La Vie du Rail

**Above: Banner of the Victor Emmanuel
Company, the railway that operated in
Savoy and Piedmont. Right: An Italian
hydraulic signal box on a station
platform. The hard physical work of
pulling signal levers was first
alleviated by a hydraulic signal box
designed by Riccardo Bianchi in 1886.**

Foto F.S.

SASSONIA

Arlberg tunnel, nearly six and a half miles long, and the Italian king, Umberto I, not to be outdone perhaps, created him a count in 1894. Ceconi went on to build other great works, such as the Podbrdo tunnel in Yugoslavia, and died still almost illiterate, having held the details of all his enterprises in his head throughout his life.

French take-over

Sicily was not forgotten in the railway boom of the 1860s. Eight miles of track from Palermo, the principal city, to Bagheria were opened on April 28, 1863. This event was an oblique product of the war against Austria. In return for his help, Napoleon demanded that Savoy and the province of Nice should be ceded to France. At the time, the Victor Emmanuel Company — named after the King of Piedmont, later King of Italy — was operating railways in both Savoy and Piedmont as well as financing the Mont Cenis tunnel. When Savoy was ceded, the Victor Emmanuel Company lines were taken over by the Paris, Lyons & Mediterranean Railway of France. France also assumed responsibility for half the cost of financing the tunnel. This left the Victor Emmanuel Company much reduced in importance as a railway operator, but, as a result of compensation, with plenty of money in the bank.

The company therefore decided to sell its remaining interests to the Piedmont State Railways and move south to Calabria and Sicily where it could profit from the government subsidy scheme by building new railways. The Palermo-Bagheria section, along a coastal plain, proved straightforward. From that point, however, construction proved increasingly difficult because of the nature of the terrain, the lack of skilled labour and the debilitating effects of malaria (from the Italian for 'bad air', which was thought to cause the disease). In the year 1872, for example, nearly 11 000 men gave up their jobs on railway construction in Calabria and Sicily because they had contracted malaria and more than 7000 left out of fear of catching the disease.

Failure by the contractors to keep to completion dates, and the consequent inability of the Victor Emmanuel Company to collect the government subsidy for routes open to traffic, placed the company under constant financial stress. At the beginning of 1867, when the first train steamed into Catania, only just over 92 miles of line had been completed with rather more than 300 miles in various stages of construction.

End of the line

Income was below operating costs on the lines open, and, in the course of the year, it proved impossible to open any more lines. There was therefore no further government subsidy forthcoming and, in 1868, the Victor Emmanuel Company finally went bankrupt. It was another 14 years before the 395 miles of north-south and east-west lines were completed as originally envisaged.

By the end of the 1870s, both the Upper Italy and Roman companies had also gone bankrupt. The Southern Railroad, with its north-south route along the shores of the Adriatic, was making a profit, however, and it was concluded that this happy situation had arisen because the company's main line ran north and south rather than across the country east-west.

Therefore two new systems — the Medi-

terranean and the Adriatic, operating on opposite sides of the Apennine Mountains — were set up in 1885, each company being granted 20-year concessions. The problems of Italian railways defied a purely geographical solution, however. Both companies, and a third formed to run the railways in Sicily, found themselves facing financial difficulties which led eventually to the formation of *Ferrovie dello Stato,* the Italian state railway system, in 1905.

Ringing the changes

A significant technical milestone in the story of Italian railways was the use, for the first time in Europe, of the telephone as a means of train operation. This was initially an American innovation, introduced in January 1882, for trains despatched between Schenectady and Ravena. Within a few months the Mediterranean System had re-signalled its Porta Nuova terminus in Turin with British-type signals and Saxby & Farmer interlockings and was also using the telephone. The man in charge of the telegraph transmitted his orders by word of mouth to an outlying junction signal box.

Up to this time the signalman had had to use his strength on levers to pull off signals and to change pairs of points. Riccardo Bianchi, signal engineer of the Mediterranean System, designed the first power signal box, using hydraulics, which was installed at Abbiategrasso, near Milan, in 1886. The signalman used miniature levers and the work was done by hydraulic power.

Hydraulic signal boxes had a vogue for a time in other countries, including France and Britain, but probably the few still in use in Italy are the only ones now operating.

Mediterranean System locomotive No. 4301 'Sassona' (Saxony) was built in 1887. The old mountain-climbing articulated Engerth and modified Engerth locomotives evolved in Austria to this tender-locomotive design by the end of the 1860s. The type was imported into Italy where it was built for many years.

ITALY GOES ELECTRIC

In 1890, Italy had three major railway companies — the Mediterranean System (RM), the Adriatic System (RA) and the Sicilian System (RS) — which had been set up by the government five years earlier. This step had been taken in the hope of achieving greater efficiency and a financial stability that the previous network of smaller companies, whether state-run or privately-owned, had rarely managed to achieve.

The law establishing the RM, RA and RS ran to more than 2000 pages and dealt, either in detail or broad principle, with every aspect of running a railway. Ownership of the infrastructure remained with the government while the three companies were responsible for operation and maintenance.

The Italians, needing more locomotives for the war, sent a design to America to be manufactured there. The final result (below) had many American features, and was most useful in both World Wars. Italian railway and tram tickets from the 1890s (right).

735.001

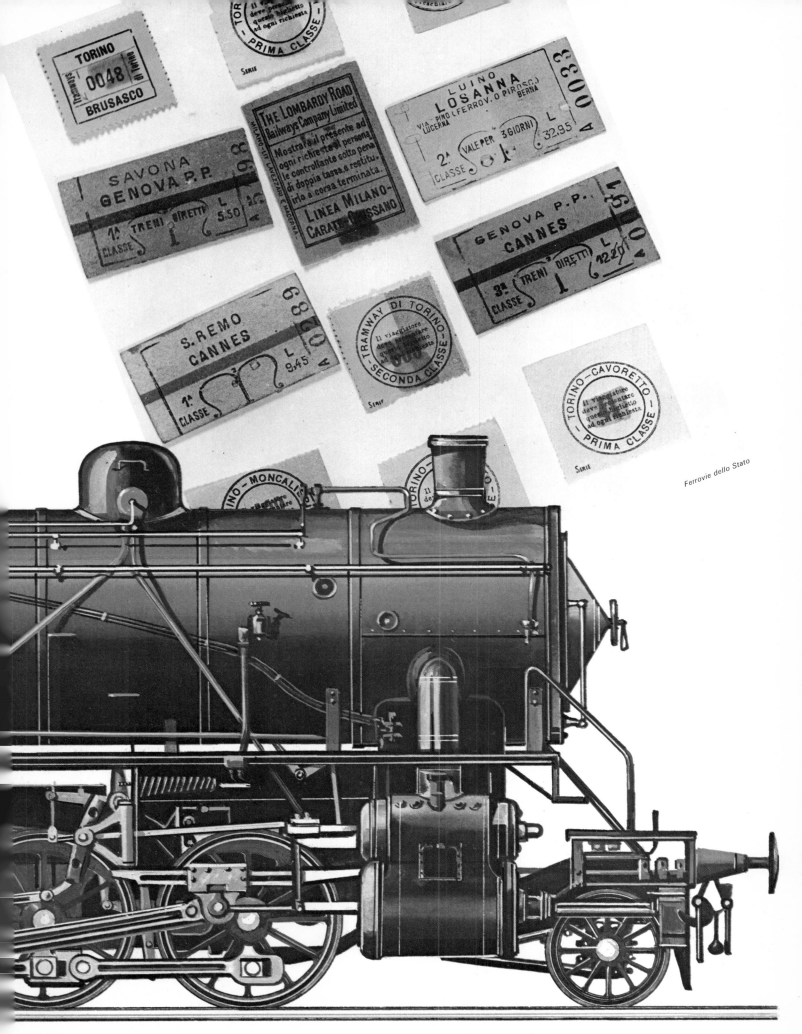

Ferrovie dello Stato

Ferrovie dello Stato

The law made provision for a uniform system of fares and freight rates as well as for through fares, which had not been available under the fragmented system existing up to that time. A railway inspectorate was also set up under the Ministry of Public Works.

Originally, the plan was to grant the three companies a 60-year concession to run their respective routes. At the last minute, however, the period was reduced to only 20 years, a decision that was to result in nationalization of the Italian railways in 1905.

Three Italian lines

The systems which each company inherited were in need of considerable improvement. Speed of construction had been the main consideration in the early days of railway expansion. The permanent way — mostly single track — therefore tended to be poorly laid and many of its curves were formidable.

In 1890, Italy's fastest train averaged only 30mph, including stops, and the 288-mile journey from Taranto to Reggio di Calabria in the toe of the country took an exhausting 16 hours at an average speed of a mere 17mph.

Apart from the state of the permanent way, lack of adequate repair and servicing facilities for locomotives did nothing to add to the speed and reliability of services. Nor was

passenger rolling stock — nearly all four-wheeled or six-wheeled coaches — very sophisticated.

A typical coach of the period was a third-class carriage built for the Calabria-Sicilian Railway in 1874. It had four wheels and carried 50 passengers in five compartments, separated by half-partitions. The seats in the compartments were only 1ft 5in (43cm) wide and, at night, the whole coach was lit by just two oil lamps.

Actually, third-class passengers on Italian main lines had to make do with wooden seats until 1932 and they are still widely used today in second-class coaches in secondary services, although it should be said that, on a stifling summer's day, with the temperature around 38°C (100°F) it can be a welcome relief not to have to sit on upholstery.

All three companies continued with policies of improvement and expansion once they took over. The RM was able to offer a better service on the improved Rome-Naples main line from 1892 and a more direct route to Sicily with the completion of a final section of a line from Battipaglia, south of Naples, to Reggio Calabria in 1895.

The RA filled in gaps on the map with branch lines which frequently ran through arid, stony, inhospitable country where the ancient custom of building townships on

steep hilltops to make them secure from marauding bands and malarial mosquitoes resulted in the new railway stations often being miles from the communities they were intended to serve. Whatever the social benefits, the commercial viability of many of these lines was dubious.

In Sicily, the RS opened a south coast line between Licata and Syracuse in 1893 and a more direct north coast line between Messina and Palermo in 1895.

Alps and Apennines

From the mid-1890s, both the RM and the RA were also beginning to put a higher standard of passenger coach into service, although not in any large quantities. They were first- and second-class bogie coaches which had side corridors, entrances and lavatories at each end, and steam-heating, an additional comfort which began to appear at about that time. The most interesting Italian innovations of the period at the turn of the century, however, concerned traction, both steam and electric.

The topography of Italy, with the great sweep of the Alps across its northern frontiers and the Apennine chain running down the centre of the country, means that it has never been a paradise for railway engineers. Even today, when most of the errors of the past

Wagons-Lits Co.

Italy's first electric railway service was provided by the battery railcar (below right) in 1899, running on the Mediterranean System between Milan and Monza, in competition with an electric tram. A suburban service between Milan and Gallarate was opened in 1901 (left). The following year work began erecting the overhead wires on the world's first high voltage electric railway (right) between Lecco, Lake Como and Sondrio.

When the electrified railway through the Simplon tunnel was opened in 1906 (below left), only three electric locomotives were available, one is to the far left in the photograph. Thus the Milan-Paris express, seen here at Iselle, Italy, was taken through the 12-mile tunnel by a Swiss steam locomotive.

have been put right, it is a country of long, steep gradients, winding routes and many tunnels. In fact, more than one mile in 20 of Italy's railway system is buried in more than 1800 tunnels.

It was not until 1890 that Italy began to build locomotives of its own distinctive design. Until that time, it had looked abroad, naturally enough to countries which had to cope with similar terrain.

Italy's first really successful mountain locomotive was an 0-8-0 built by Wiener Neustadt of Austria for the Upper Italy Railways in 1873. By 1885, the Upper Italy had 106 locomotives of this type, which were divided between the RM and RA in the government-enforced amalgamation of companies. RM went on building these 0-8-0s until 1905 and some remained in service for nearly half a century, 10 surviving until after 1950.

One recurring problem that faced Italian railway operators was the haulage of freight in and out of the growing port of Genoa. The first railway route to the port, which is surrounded by steep hills, had been the Giovi incline, four and a half miles long with a crippling 1:28½ gradient. By the mid-1880s, a less demanding relief route, the *succursale*, was under construction, 14½ miles long and starting at the Genoa end with the more modest gradient of 1:62.

Ferrovie dello Stato

Ferrovie dello Stato

per l'INAUGURAZIONE della I: FERROVIA ELETTRICA in ITALIA

R

CORSE ELETTRICHE

MILANO
2 - 8 - 99
M
MONZA

FRA MILANO E MONZA

To deal with traffic on the difficult Giovi inclines, Italy had Europe's first 4-6-0 locomotive, built in 1884 and given the name *Vittorio Emanuele II*. This was followed in 1902 by Europe's first 4-8-0, both products of the RM locomotive design office which had been set up in Turin.

In all, 40 of these two-cylinder compound 4-8-0s were built, but proved something of a flop from the start, for they were not powerful enough for the job. Another flaw was that, beneath their Wootten firebox, they had a shallow ashpan which quickly filled up and choked a large part of the grate.

After a short time, they were taken off the Giovi runs, modified and used to work trains up from Domodossola to the Simplon tunnel. This task, too, proved rather beyond their powers. Like many Italian locomotives, however, they had a gift for survival and continued to operate on the undemanding plains around Venice until the early 1930s.

Italy electrified

The problem posed by the Giovi inclines was not just the steep gradients, but the fact that steam locomotives filled the many tunnels with choking smoke. The number of trains allowed to pass during each hour had therefore to be severely restricted. Electric traction eventually solved both difficulties, but only after a delay of several years and another upheaval in Italian railway organization.

Italians have made many contributions to increasing human knowledge about electricity and applying that knowledge for the benefit of mankind: Guglielmo Marconi is acknowledged as the father of radio communication; Alessandro Volta gave his name to the volt; Luigi Galvani gave his to the galvanizing process. It is therefore not surprising that Italy led the way in the large-scale electrification of railways.

Antonio Pacinotti, an Italian whose name is less familiar, had pointed out the path as early as 1860 by making the first dynamo and recognizing that, in reverse, it was an electric motor. The first electric tramway in the country started in Florence in 1890, the first railway

An Italian State Railway's 680 Class locomotive in 1914 (left).
A 'Pacific' type locomotive (below) was used by the Italian State Railways to haul express passenger trains from Milan to Venice and from Milan south to Florence and as far as Chiusi on the route to Rome.

service beginning operations nine years later between Milan and Monza.

On February 8, 1899, the RM inaugurated a service of 22 trains a day, using two battery railcars which could carry 24 first-class passengers, 40 second-class passengers and 24 standing passengers. Power was provided by accumulators which weighed 18 tons and had sufficient capacity for two round trips, a total of 38 miles, before they had to be re-charged.

The RA began an accumulator railcar service on the 27-mile route between Bologna and San Felice on May 1 of the same year. The accumulators were much smaller on this service, weighing only eight tons, and had to be recharged at the beginning and end of each journey.

Performance proved erratic, mainly because of the inadequacy of the accumulators, and both services were scrapped by the end of 1904.

Two other electrification schemes were already in use at this time. The RM, using a third rail to provide the power, electrified 36 route-miles from Milan to Varese, close to the Swiss frontier, in October 1901. Three months earlier, the RA had opened a trial service over the 16-mile line between Colico, on the shore of Lake Como, and Chiavenna in the Alpine foothills, using high-voltage, three-phase DC with its two familiar overhead wires.

The trial proved so successful that the RA proceeded to electrify another 49 miles by the same system, starting at Lecco, farther south on Lake Como, running to Colico and then to Sondrio in the Alpine foothills to the east. The original Colico-Chiavenna route thus became a branch line of this longer section of electrification.

Public services began on both lines on October 15, 1902, amid great excitement, the Italians ignoring the fact that the same system was already in use between Bergdorf and Thun in Switzerland and claiming an international 'first'.

The coaches – there were two types, one carrying 24 first-class passengers and their luggage, the other 24 first-class passengers and 32 second-class – were worthy of the innovation with their ornate decor, rich carpets, gilt armchairs and occasional tables set beneath windows which boasted Venetian blinds as well as curtains.

As early as 1898 it had become clear that the RM, RA and RS were not making a better job of running the railways, in terms of profitability and service to the public, than the smaller companies they had replaced. A government commission appointed to look into the whole question produced an ambiguous report, recommending on the one hand that the concessions of the three companies should be renewed in 1905, and on the other that there should be closer government supervision.

The Italian traveller showed himself increasingly in favour of nationalization, a method of railway operation already working successfully in other countries. Another important group, railway workers, also gave strong support to this course of action because they felt their pay and conditions were more likely to improve under the state.

Nationalised

In 1903 the government announced its decision: the concessions to RM, RA and RS would not be renewed and Italy's railways would pass into the control of the state. In order to salvage as much cash as they could for shareholders, the three companies promptly abandoned schemes involving capital outlay and, as far as possible, instituted a wage freeze a policy that led to a bitter railway strike early in 1905.

The *Ferrovie dello Stato* (Italian State Railways) began operations on July 1, 1905, with Riccardo Bianchi, former general manager of the Sicilian system, as the first director general. He faced a task which, like so many miles of Italian track, was mainly uphill.

The railways were run-down and morale among the workers low. Large numbers of locomotives had reached the end of their useful life and were fit only for scrapping. Of the passenger coaches he had taken over – only 116 with bogies against 6717 four-wheelers and six-wheelers – many needed extensive servicing while others were out of action because of defects. At the same time, servicing and repair facilities were inadequate, both for locomotives and rolling stock. Furthermore, the country had only 1187 miles of double-track line.

Bianchi's first year in office was not made any easier by a series of natural disasters. An earthquake in Reggio Calabria was followed in December 1905 by extensive floods. Four months later Vesuvius erupted and caused chaos: fine ash from the volcano masking signals and choking wheel bearings.

On a more cheerful note, Bianchi was able to report that he had ordered 567 new locomotives, 1244 new passenger coaches and 20 623 new freight wagons. All of the new passenger coaches would have bogies, steam heating, air brakes and electric lighting. The side-corridor coaches would carry either 42 first-class passengers, served by two lavatories, or 79 third-class passengers, served by one lavatory, although, in the case of holders of third-class tickets, 'lavatory' was a somewhat dignified name for what was basically a hole in the floor.

A start was made in 1908 on the task, usually formidable, of increasing the country's mileage of double track. Work began on both the Florence-Rome and Genoa-La Spezia routes. The degree of difficulty posed by the terrain can be judged by the time it took to complete these two operations. The double-track line between Florence and Rome was not open until 1933 and between Genoa and La Spezia – where 34 of the 57 miles are under ground and there are 14 major viaducts – not until 1970.

Increased traffic in and out of the port of Genoa was again a problem in the early years of Bianchi's reign on the FS. One plan mooted was to build yet a third incline at astronomical expense. Instead, Bianchi chose to try out the three-phase electrification system which had proved so successful on the Lecco-Colico-Sondrio route.

The original Giovi incline, with its punishing gradients, was electrified on August 1, 1910, and an E550 locomotive, built by Ganz and Co. of Budapest, made light of hauling a 400-ton load up to the summit at a steady 28mph. As it was only half the size of the giant steam locomotives which had previously laboured to perform the same task, the E550 has passed into the folklore of Italian railways as *il piccolo gigante dei Giovi* (the little giant of the Giovi).

The second incline, the *succursale,* was electrified in 1914. A bonus in both cases was the reduction of smoke nuisance in the tunnels which until then had seriously reduced the frequency of trains. In broader terms, the success of electric traction on the first of the Giovi inclines demonstrated beyond argument that the three-phase DC system was ideally suited at that period for main-line electrification.

As early as 1912 it had been adopted on the 1:36 approaches to the Mont Cenis tunnel on the Italian side, and by 1915 the line was electrified right through the tunnel to Modane. E550s hauled the trains and, in all, 186 electric locomotives of this type were built by Italiana-Westinghouse between 1908 and 1921. It is only fitting that one should be preserved in the Leonardo da Vinci Museum of Science and Technology at Milan.

The Italian State Railways ordered 186 of these ten-coupled locomotives (right) between 1908 and 1921. They were designed by the Hungarian Kálmán Kandó for work on Italy's newly electrified mountain railways. They earned the nickname 'Little Giants of Giovi' for their work on the Giovi pass north of Genoa. The architectural department of the old Mediterranean System designed Genoa station in the French Renaissance style (top). It was opened in 1905.

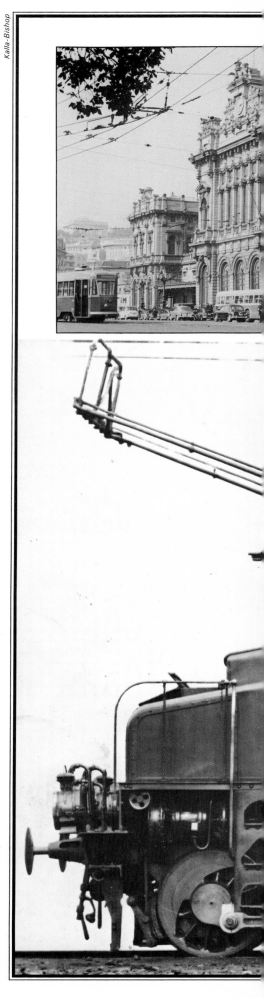

The later years of the First World War saw Italy playing host to an unusual international train, formed to duplicate Allied lines of communication with the Mediterranean. It ran from Cherbourg to Taranto via Mexidon, Tours, Lyons, the Mont Cenis tunnel, Faenza and Bari.

The 1500-mile journey took more than a week. Yet, at the peak of its use, trains were despatched on this trans-European overland route at the rate of more than two a day, and, between February 1917 when it was inaugurated and February 1919, it transported no less than 400 000 passengers and 184 000 tons of freight.

The end of the war, and the defeat of Austria, brought Italy 779 route-miles of new railway in ceded territory, including 292 miles of the old Südbahn. The major route involved was the Brenner Pass line. Needless to say, it was all uphill, to the village of Brenner at the summit.

Kalla-Bishop

TRACKS ACROSS

The United States had its first steam locomotives from England in 1828, but they were not successful as they were too heavy for the lightly-laid track. Horses were therefore the accepted motive power until 1830 when the inventor Peter Cooper produced the first American-built locomotive, named *Tom Thumb* because it was so small.

Tom Thumb made its first public appearance on August 25, 1830, on a 13-mile length of double track between Baltimore and Ellicott's Mills. It covered the outward journey in the highly respectable time of one hour, but, on the return trip, developed a mechanical fault and suffered the humiliation of being caught and passed by a horse-drawn 'train' on the adjoining track.

Nevertheless, *Tom Thumb* had done enough to indicate the potential of the railroad. This view was reinforced by events down in South Carolina. On January 15, 1831, pretty girls strewed flowers on the track when the locomotive named *Best Friend of Charleston* took over from the horse on the first section of the South Carolina Railroad (forerunner of the Southern Railway), which had been opened in 1829. The *Best Friend of Charleston* provided a regular 20-mph service between that city and neighbouring towns for six months until the fireman, apparently irritated by the hiss of escaping steam, fastened down the locomotive's safety valve.

The resulting violent explosion, which demolished Charleston's *Best Friend*, was held to be the fault of man rather than the machine and did nothing to diminish the

enthusiasm for this new form of locomotion. The year 1831 also saw the Camden & Amboy in New Jersey (connecting New York with Philadelphia and later incorporated in the great Pennsylvania Railroad) open its first section with steam traction, while the Mohawk & Hudson Rail Road began operations between Albany and Schenectady, the first section of what was to become the New York Central System.

Expansion without expense

The next 30 years saw a proliferation of lines, from north to south and even west as far as the Mississippi and Missouri rivers. The railway had come to the United States when it was still largely an agricultural country of scattered communities. The capital available was used to link these communities, and unify the country, as rapidly as possible without concern for a solid road-bed, gentle curves, expensive tunnels or grandiose stations.

"No one worries much about choosing the shortest route . . ." wrote Jules Verne. " . . . The line goes up hillsides, scrambles down into valleys, and runs along blindly and rarely in a straight line." Cows on the track were a regular hazard; derailments were frequent, passengers being invited to step down to help put the vehicle back in position; and sparks from wood-burning locomotives posed a constant threat to fields and crops.

Isaac Dripp, master mechanic of the Camden & Amboy, is generally held to have invented the locomotive pilot — known in Britain as a 'cowcatcher' — in about 1830 to clear stray cattle from the line, and bogies,

AMERICA

The very first American-built locomotive was the 'Tom Thumb' (left), seen here in a race against a horse-drawn coach in 1830 outside Baltimore. 'Tom Thumb' lost. Robert Stephenson & Company built the 'John Bull' (below) for the Camden & Amboy Railroad, New Jersey, in 1831. The master mechanic on the railroad, Isaac Dripp, is supposed to have invented the locomotive pilot, known as the 'cowcatcher'; this and the leading pair of wheels are the American additions to the original locomotive.
Right: A timetable of 1840 issued by the Baltimore & Susquehanna Railroad.

A stove is provided for the passengers on the Baltimore & Ohio Railroad (left). One of the most difficult sections of the Union Pacific was the grading of the track at Weber Canyon (right). Each shelf was hacked out of the rock, then pick-axed and blasted down to the level. Temporary tracks took away rubble on the lower levels, while mules and carts were used on the upper stages. The colourful American Express train (below), in a Currier and Ives print, has the four-coupled locomotive with a four-wheel truck leading the carriages, a characteristic arrangement of the period. The first purpose-built sleeping car was produced by George Mortimer Pullman (far right) in 1865, and the first American restaurant car three years later.

a pivoting arrangement of four small wheels, were also used very early to guide the front of locomotives along the rough tracks and promote good riding.

Crude bogies had been employed occasionally on colliery tramroads in England and Robert Stephenson is credited with suggesting to American engineers that they might help to overcome the difficult conditions in the United States. The first locomotive in the world with a leading bogie was the *Experiment*, later called *Brother Jonathan*, for the Mohawk & Hudson in 1832.

By the 1840s, three great lines were pressing west — New York to the Great Lakes and beyond; Baltimore to St Louis; Richmond to Memphis — and a line from north to south linked Chicago with the Gulf of Mexico. The typical American-type locomotive had been developed, with four coupled driving wheels, outside cylinders, a leading four-wheel bogie, and, where wood was used as fuel, a vast spark-arrester chimney.

Winter warmth

The familiar American passenger car — long and mounted on bogies, although lacking the clerestory on the roof, which was adopted a little later to give better ventilation — was also in use. The interior was arranged as one saloon with a central aisle for the practical reason that, in hard American winters, the whole coach could be heated by a couple of stoves placed at either end. A lavatory at each end of the car was a feature from the 1860s.

As one chronicler has put it, the railway in these early years had a dramatic impact on a country of largely isolated communities and "gave the signal for an advance of civilization without parallel. When, for example, the great north to south line was built across the prairies, no settler could remain a hermit. Behind the fence, farms, factories, shops, inns and warehouses grew like mushrooms."

But the country beyond the Mississippi and Missouri rivers remained a hostile, sparsely-populated wilderness and there were many influential voices quite happy to leave it like that. "What do we want with this region of savages and wild beasts, of deserts, of shifting sands and whirlwinds of dust, of cactus and prairie dogs?" asked Daniel Webster, the illustrious senator from Mas-

sachusetts, in 1845. "To what use could we ever put those endless mountain ranges? . . . What could we do with the western coast line three thousand miles away, rockbound, cheerless and uninviting?"

On the other hand there was a strong feeling that, unless there was some easy, cheap and rapid means of communicating with these remote parts of the country, there was a great danger that they might be lost to the Union. Even with the Pony Express — 400 mustangs and a force of riders who changed mounts every 20 or 25 miles — it took 13 days for written matter to cover the 1600 miles between California and Missouri.

Meeting halfway

Finally, after several conflicting surveys had been made, President Abraham Lincoln put an end to the argument in the midst of the Civil War by signing the Pacific Railroad Act of 1862. Two companies were to be involved in building the line, the Central Pacific from California and the Union Pacific from Omaha, and they would meet at a point to be determined by their speed of progress.

The CP was granted 10 miles of land in alternate sections on either side of each mile of track laid, plus loans of $16 000 a mile on the plains, $32 000 through the Great Basin, and $48 000 over the difficult Rocky and Sierra Mountains. The UP enjoyed the same general conditions.

It was expected that the task of building the railroad would take 14 years. In fact, it was completed in six — despite floods, blizzards with 40ft snowdrifts, avalanches, unstable explosives, collapsed bridges, temperatures so low that tools shattered, marauding Indians, torrid deserts, lack of water, violent storms on the plains, shortage of labour, and the inevitable disruptive camp followers, eager to supply whisky, painted women and other facilities designed to take a man's mind off his work.

Initially, the CP faced the toughest going, the peaks of the Sierras being only 70 miles from Sacramento, starting point of the west-east line. The company advertised throughout California for 5000 workers, but rarely had more than 800 on its books, and scores of those disappeared each pay day to squander their money in bars or brothels or to seek their fortune in the Nevada silver mines.

The Union Pacific Railroad imported Chinese labour to build their tracks; they worked phenomenally hard and put the other navvies to shame. Left is a Chinese section gang in Promontory, Utah, in about 1869. The Union Pacific's photographic car is in the background. Towns sprang up and vanished within a few months of the railroad being finished. Bear River City (right) was a typical example of these 'Hells on Wheels', although when this photograph was taken the town boasted 200 inhabitants.
The encampment at Dale Creek Bridge (below) looks even more temporary. The bridge structure is typical of the timber trestles used throughout the American West.

The man in charge of construction at this end of the line was James Harvey Strobridge, a 37-year-old New England man with a talent for cursing and a justified reputation as a slave driver. He looked upon the workers under his control as 'near brutes' and summed up his attitude to labour relations in the laconic sentence: "Men generally earn their money when they work for me." Itinerant whisky peddlers, who made their way out to the railhead, rarely made the journey twice because, on Strobridge's orders, their stock was seized and smashed before they could sell it — and they received no compensation.

Chinese labour

An attempt to solve the CP's labour shortage led to the recruitment of 50 Chinese immigrants, a move resisted by Strobridge, who looked upon them as frail and inferior beings, given to such bizarre habits as wearing pigtails and eating cuttlefish, bamboo shoots and seaweed. His misgivings proved unfounded. The Chinese, who brought their own cooks and paid them themselves, turned out to be prodigious and courageous workers who, if anything, put to shame the hefty Irish immigrants, Civil War veterans, freed slaves and occasional Indians working alongside them.

They went in fear of Strobridge, whom they called 'One Eye Bossy Man' because he had lost an eye in an explosion, but it was their naturally disciplined habits which ensured that, although fond of the occasional pipe of opium, they never slacked, never got drunk and never slipped off to sample the pleasures of mining towns along the route. These admirable qualities made them so popular that, by the middle of 1865, nearly every able-bodied man in the Chinatowns of Sacramento and San Francisco had been recruited by the railroad and further reinforcements had to be imported from China itself.

The other factor which promised to make the conquest of the mountains easier for the CP was the new European invention, nitroglycerin. Imports of the powerful explosive were virtually banned in California, however, after two crates of it blew up in San Francisco, killing 12 bystanders and sending a severed arm hurtling through a third-storey window. Strobridge overcame that

difficulty by having the three basic ingredients — glycerin, nitric acid and sulphuric acid — brought in separately and employing a Scottish chemist named James Howden to mix a daily supply of the dangerous, unstable concoction in a special workshop built high in the Sierras.

Away to the east, a similar UP army, strung out across 500 miles of plains, pushed ever westward. First came the surveyors; then — as much as 300 miles ahead of the main force — the graders, laying the roadbed; behind them, the bridge monkeys; and finally the work train with tools, a blacksmith's shop, boxcars housing several hundred men in tiers of bunks, tents on the roofs and hammocks slung underneath, a kitchen, a storeroom and an office.

The scene when the work train came to life at the start of a new day was described by a reporter from the *New York Evening Post* in 1867: "It is half-past five and time for the hands to be waked up. This is done by ringing a bell on the sleeping car until everyone turns out and by giving the fellows under the car a smart kick and by pelting the fellows in the tents on the top with bits of clay.

"In a very few minutes they are all out, stretching and yawning. Another bell and they crowd in for breakfast. The table is lighted by hanging lamps, for it is yet hardly daylight. At intervals of about a yard are wooden buckets of coffee, great plates of bread and platters of meat. There is no ceremony: every man dips his cup into the buckets of coffee and sticks his own fork into whatever is nearest him . . ."

Camp followers

The UP took a more tolerant attitude than Strobridge to camp followers. Tented towns populated largely by saloon keepers, gamblers and ladies of easy virtue mushroomed every 50 miles or so along the track, were given names (Julesburg, Cheyenne, Laramie) and then abandoned as the railroad stretched ever farther towards the setting sun.

Henry Stanley, the journalist later sent to find Dr Livingstone, was despatched by the *New York Tribune* to report on the scene and was shocked in particular by the harlots of the makeshift towns. "These women," he wrote, "are expensive articles and come in for a large share of the money wasted. In

broad daylight they may be seen gliding through the dusty streets carrying fancy derringers slung to their waists, with which tools they are dangerously expert. Western chivalry will not allow them to be abused by any man they may have robbed. Mostly everyone seemed bent on debauchery and dissipation.''

The crossing of the plains brought conflict with the fierce Sioux and many of the Cheyenne tribes, who refused to be placated by offers of free rail travel for life. At first, unable to grasp the power of locomotives, they attacked them with bows and arrows and tried to derail them with lariats strung across the tracks. In one incident, involving a war party of 50 braves split into two parties on either side of the track, a locomotive ploughed into the lariats at 25mph, dragged several Indians and their ponies under its wheels and cut them to pieces.

Indians on the warpath

However, the Indians soon learned the more sophisticated techniques of cutting telegraph lines and causing derailments, a development which earned an unwelcome niche in the folklore of the Far West for a young Englishman named William Thompson. After the telegraph line near Plum Creek went dead on a night in August 1867, Thompson set out with five other men on a hand-pump car to locate the fault.

They did not know that a party of Cheyenne, led by a chief named Turkey Leg, had torn down the telegraph wire and used it to lash a barrier of loose sleepers to the track. The hand-pump car crashed into the barrier and, within a few seconds, the fair-haired Thompson — clubbed down and scalped — was the only member of the repair party still alive.

As he lay on the ground, he saw his blonde locks fall from the belt of the brave who had scalped him. He managed to retrieve them in the darkness and staggered off towards Plum Creek, hoping to find a doctor who could stitch his hair back on for him. At Plum Creek, where he eventually arrived safely, it was decided that more sophisticated medical talents were needed than could be found locally, and Thompson, with his scalp in a bucket of water, was despatched by special train to Omaha, 250 miles to the east.

There, a Dr Moore came to the conclusion that Thompson's scalp was so badly mutilated that there was no point in trying to restore it to its rightful place. Thompson, once recovered, returned to railroading and became a much-admired figure, one of many railwaymen condemned to instant baldness in the course of winning the West. He also appears to have borne no resentment over Dr Moore's decision not to try to sew his

Top: The poster announcing the grand opening of the Union Pacific Railroad. Left: Perhaps the most famous railway photograph ever taken — the scene at Promontory Point, Utah, when the Union Pacific rails from the east met those built from the west coast. Shaking hands are the two chief engineers, Grenville M. Dodge for U.P. and Samuel S. Montague for C.P.

Union Pacific

scalp back into place because he later had it tanned and sent it to the doctor as a souvenir.

The Army's response to these and other attacks was to send 5000 soldiers to guard the UP track and the men working on it. As effective in the end, however, was the decision to soften up the Indians with liberal supplies of free whisky. This generosity turned them by the hundred into whisky addicts, more interested in laying hands on a jug of firewater than combating the threat which the railroad – and the hordes of settlers who would follow – posed to their traditional homelands and the buffalo on which they relied so heavily for meat.

The last spike

So the two tracks pushed ahead, sometimes two miles a day, sometimes five – and on one occasion, to settle a bet, a historic 10 miles – until, in May 1869, the lines finally met in the desolate wastes of Utah. The masterminds of the two companies, Leland Stanford of CP and Thomas Durant of UP, were to signal completion of the transcontinental route by the ceremonial driving of the last iron spike. Unfortunately, unused to wielding heavy hammers, they both missed at the first attempt. Nevertheless, the telegraph operator sent the signal: "Done." In California, celebratory cannon were fired and there was dancing in the streets: the West was linked at last with the 30 000 or more miles of track already operating in the East.

West of the Missouri, however, rail travel was still a risky business. There was always the possibility of being incinerated in a prairie fire, begun accidentally by sparks from a locomotive or deliberately by hostile Indians . . . or being fleeced by cardsharps . . . or being robbed by bandits.

Gambling madam

'Poker' Alice – a slim, English-born beauty with fair hair, blue eyes and rosy cheeks – was one of the legendary cardsharps who worked the trains from time to time as a kind of vacation from her normal place of business, the gaming tables of the mining camps. She eventually amassed enough money to retire to Deadwood, South Dakota, where she opened a celebrated brothel which managed to combine the customary services to the community with strict observance of the Sabbath. On Sundays, men and cards were banned and 'Poker' Alice gave bible lessons to the ladies of the establishment.

George Devol, another legendary gambler, is estimated to have relieved fellow travellers of $2 million, using a marked deck. Devol, who had an exceptionally hard skull, frequently silenced protesting victims, who had caught him cheating, by butting them, and he once butted a man so hard that he killed him. He was also regularly involved in shootouts. Nevertheless, he survived these miscellaneous adventures to die penniless.

Canada Bill Jones is another gambler who deserves his place in history if only on the grounds of initiative. When UP was threatening to ban cardsharps, he offered the company $10 000 for a 12-month concession to work the trains, promising to confine his victims to travelling salesmen and Methodist preachers. UP turned him down.

Another, although less costly, cause of irritation in these early days was the recurrent need to change trains. Through-running was not possible over the majority of routes. The northern states, under English influence, had adopted standard gauge of 4ft 8½in. The new transcontinental railroad was also standard. Elsewhere, however, a wide variety of gauges – 5ft in the south, 5ft 6in in Texas, 6ft between New York and Lake Erie – had come into being until, by the middle of the century, there were no fewer than 12. Congress then decreed that all should be converted to standard gauge.

The task took time. The 5ft track running 500 miles from Cairo, Illinois, to New Orleans, was not converted to standard gauge until 1881 although, to give the company credit, once they got around to the job they completed it in a single day. The last of the American broad-gauge lines in service was the 5ft road running inland from Savannah, Georgia, which was finally converted in 1886.

Technical refinements

Technically, two important American contributions to railway operation and safety were the perfection by Samuel Morse of his telegraph code in 1844 and the invention by George Westinghouse of the automatic air brake, patented in 1869.

The electric telegraph had first been tried out on the London & Birmingham Railway

Philadelphia & Reading No. 411 (below) was a typical American locomotive in an unusual guise: the boiler was designed to burn anthracite coal dust which normally went to waste. In order to burn the fuel the Wootten firebox was of exceptional width and area, but this prevented the engineer seeing round it. He was therefore given a cab above the boiler – hence the nickname

'camelbacks' for these locomotives. No. 143 was built in 1880 and gave a good account of itself, attaining 77mph on trials. A meeting of Union Pacific's board of directors (above right), about 1869. Thomas C. Durant the president is flanked to his right by Sidney Dillon and to his left by John Duff, each in turn later to become presidents of the railroad.

George Westinghouse (left) introduced the air brake, which allowed the whole train to be braked from the locomotive cab. If the carriages were to become uncoupled, separate parts of the train would be automatically brought to a halt. The Canadian railroad system developed slowly from a 15-mile line in 1836. In 1884 the first transcontinental Canadian Pacific Railway train arrived at Port Moody (right), crossing Canada by rail for the first time. The engine, No. 373, was built in the Company's workshops in Montreal. A year later the rails were extended to Vancouver. The last spike was driven in at Craigellachie, Eagle Pass in the Rocky Mountains on November 7 (below right) by Donald A. Smith (later Lord Strathcona).

in 1837. Outside Britain, the electric telegraph, in conjunction with the Morse Code, had a major effect on railroad operation, ready communication allowing swift decisions to be made between dispatchers at each station as to which train was to occupy a single track section. As early as 1851, when the Erie Railroad was completed, it was equipped with a dispatching system throughout its 469-mile length.

The Westinghouse air brake, which allowed the whole train to be braked from the locomotive cab and ensured that, in the event of a snapped coupling, both parts of the train would be brought to a halt automatically, was standard in the United States almost from the 1870s. But in Europe there was confusion. In England in 1890, for instance, two of the four railway companies running south of London had chosen the air brake while the other two had chosen the vacuum brake. Eventually, but not until the 1920s, the air brake was standardized in continental Europe, but as this is being written British Rail is still in the middle of changing from the vacuum to the air brake.

The United States also produced the man whose name was to become synonymous throughout his native country and Britain with luxury in rail travel, George Mortimer Pullman, who produced the world's first purpose-built sleeping car in 1865; the United States' first specialized restaurant car, the *Delmonico,* named after a top-class New York restaurant in 1868; and also devised corridor connections between coaches for passenger use in 1887.

Luxury on wheels

Most of the long-distance railroads soon handed the matter of sleeping accommodation over to the Pullman Palace Car Company, established in 1867 with 48 carriages. But, as Bryan Morgan points out in *Two Pioneers,* one of his contributions to the book *Great Trains,* "it was not only on scheduled expresses that Pullman placed his imprint, for between the 'seventies and the end of the century the ownership (or, at a pinch, the hiring) of a *private* Pullman coach, set or entire train became as much a status symbol as that of the steam-yachts from which so much of their architecture derived . . .

"They were, in fact and in the late Lucius

Beebe's words, 'mansions on rails', costing up to half a million dollars, over 90ft long and weighing nearly a hundred tons apiece. Perhaps none was ever equipped with a swimming bath like that featured in Kipling's short story . . . but this was almost the only luxury which *was* missing, and various 'private varnish' vehicles or trains boasted such conveniences and inconveniences as open grates, harmoniums, portable mushroom farms, printing presses and Jersey cattle to provide fresh milk, as well as the inevitable potted plants, acres of inlaid hardwoods, bevelled glass and bobbled plush, *epergnes* and winecoolers by the dozen, and legions of servants in full rig."

The standard of meals had reached such a high level by 1890 that travellers on the Chicago & North Western could enjoy a Christmas dinner consisting of 12 courses with a choice from 45 dishes, including green turtle soup, Californian salmon, beef, turkey stuffed with chestnuts, goose, duck, roast quail, croquettes of oysters, asparagus, English plum pudding with brandy sauce, mince and pumpkin pie, New York ice cream and Roquefort cheese.

Drama on the Pacific routes

By then, another three routes to the Pacific had been opened in the United States — the Southern Pacific and the Northern Pacific, both in 1883, and the Atchison, Topeka & Sante Fe in 1885 — and a fourth, the Great Northern, was well on the way to completion. Between the Mississippi and the Pacific, mileage had grown from a mere five miles in 1852 to more than 72 000 miles.

Each of the new routes had its dramas. The Santa Fe, for instance, was completed only after a bitter four-year running battle with the rival Denver & Rio Grande in which trestle bridges were burned to the ground, track was blown up and both sides hired gunmen by the score, the Santa Fe importing the legendary Bat Masterson from Dodge City to lead its forces. The cost of the railroad war eventually escalated to the point where financiers ordered the shooting to stop and a compromise solution was reached; the Denver & Rio Grande was given an exclusive line to the rich silver mines of Colorado while the Santa Fe pushed on into New Mexico and to the Pacific coast.

Human nature being what it is, there were also lighter moments. When the Southern Pacific reached Tucson, Arizona, in 1880, Mayor Leatherwood decided the occasion should be marked by the driving of a silver spike and the firing of a 38-gun salute. In the course of the conviviality it was decided that telegrams should be despatched to several important people informing them of this historic occasion. One of these, addressed to "The Pope, Rome, Italy," read: "The Mayor of Tucson begs to inform His Holiness that this ancient and honourable pueblo was founded by Spaniards under sanction of the Church more than 300 years ago and to inform Your Holiness that a railroad from San Francisco, California, now connects us with the Christian world. Asking your benediction."

Shortly afterwards, Mayor Leatherwood received a reply saying: "Am glad the railroad has reached Tucson, but where the hell is Tucson? The Pope." Despite the rapidity of the reply and the non-ecclesiastic language, it was some time before it dawned on the assembled dignitaries that the Southern Pacific might have a telegraph operator with a sense of humour on its payroll.

Canadian complications

To the north, Canada, which had had its first railway — an unimportant 15-mile line from St John to Laprairie — in 1836, was preoccupied with the question of a transcontinental railroad throughout the 1870s and the first half of the 1880s. Such a line had been promised in the negotiations which led to British Columbia, the Pacific coast province, becoming part of Canada in 1871.

It was a formidable undertaking. There was a thousand miles of rocky wasteland to be crossed in northern Ontario, a thousand miles of empty prairie beyond Winnipeg, and then the formidable Rockies. Furthermore, Canada was an infant country with a scattered population of only four million in contrast to the 40 million inhabitants of the United States.

The project received a serious setback in 1873 when Sir John Macdonald's government was brought down by scandal when it came to light that the chief financier of the company formed to build the railroad had contributed heavily to the costs of Macdonald's successful election campaign 12 months earlier. The collapse of the government coincided with a great depression, and it was not until Macdonald again came to power in 1878 that real impetus was given to fulfilling the pledge made to British Columbia.

The railroad company, which had been forced to ask for repeated government help, ran out of money again in 1885, and it took a rebellion to persuade the authorities that it was worth putting up the money to complete the track. The Indians were worried about the vanishing buffalo and unhappy about the terms of many of the treaties forced upon them; French-Catholics were hostile to Anglo-Protestant rule. Louis Riel, who had led a previous revolt in 1870, returned from exile in Montana to head this second rebellion whose fundamental aim was to create a separate province for Indians, French-Catholics and half-breeds.

In the ensuing struggle, the railroad demonstrated its value in moving troops quickly to points where they were needed. The rebellion was quelled and the government happily produced the money to complete the line to the Pacific coast. The last spike of the Canadian Pacific Railway was driven on November 7, 1885: nine days later, despite pleas for clemency, Riel was hanged at Regina for treason.

In both the United States and Canada, the railroad knitted together existing scattered communities and then opened up new territory for settlement. It also created the means of easy communication that were essential for national unity and future prosperity. In this sense, the history of the railroad may be said to be the history of the North American continent.

GREAT AMERICAN

The first half-century of the railroads in the United States was dominated by the opening up of the West.

Four of the great routes to the Pacific – the Union and Central Pacific, the Southern Pacific, the Northern Pacific, and the Atchison, Topeka & Santa Fe – were already operational in 1890, and the fifth, the Great Northern, was nearing completion. In the space of 25 years, mileage west of the Mississippi River had risen from 3200 miles of jumbled track to an orderly 72 000 miles, with dozens of feeder lines serving the main routes. As a result, more settlers went West between 1870 and 1900 than the total in the previous 250 years.

After the great routes came the great trains and the great locomotives to haul them, and the years between 1890 and 1920 saw speed increasingly married to the luxury which had already been pioneered by George Mortimer Pullman.

Faster giants

Higher speeds meant more power, and, given the poorer quality coal available in the United States, increased power could be achieved only by enlarging the spread of the firebox grate. Initially, designers turned from the 4-4-0s, easily the most common type of locomotive as the century came to a close, to *Atlantic* 4-4-2s whose two small trailing

wheels supported a longer locomotive without imposing restrictions on use of the space above them.

This trend was followed almost at once by *Pacific* 4-6-2s, soon widely adopted as the standard locomotive for passenger expresses. As early as 1904, the Union Pacific had a locomotive of this type which weighed nearly 100 tons without its tender and had a grate area of $49\frac{1}{2}$ square feet (most British locomotives of this period had grates of less than 20 square feet).

The UP's giant was nothing exceptional, however, when compared with some of the mammoth freight locomotives that began to appear about this time. Two factors – the

RAILROADS

continuous automatic air brake and long stretches of single track — combined to ensure that freight trains in the United States increased both in length and weight to enormous proportions.

Heaviest in the world

In 1903, the Atchison, Topeka & Santa Fe ordered no fewer than 70 of a new type of 2-10-2s from Baldwins of Philadelphia. These locomotives, which weighed 128 tons and were supplied with coal and water by tenders weighing more than 60 tons when fully loaded, were said at the time to be the heaviest locomotive class in the world, and it was necessary to re-lay miles of track in

some parts of the country before these mobile mammoths could be run with safety.

Even bigger locomotives followed — a Great Northern Mallet 2-6-6-2 of 1906 that weighed 158 tons with a 66-ton tender, and a Southern Pacific Mallet 2-8-8-2, built by Baldwins in 1908, that weighed 190 tons and had an 80-ton tender. Interestingly, these, and a long succession of freight locomotives that followed, featured an articulated adaptation of compounding principles developed by the Frenchman, Anatole Mallet, to deal with the heavy gradients and continuous curves of the St Gotthard line.

Mallet's engine for the St Gotthard line had articulated connections between the steam

Opposite, top: A Union Pacific Railroad light passenger Atlantic-type locomotive first built in 1904. The Union Pacific Railroad Pacific-type locomotive No. 3412 is seen here in its original condition (below). Inset: A Pacific locomotive for the Atchison, Topeka & Santa Fe Railway.
Anatole Mallet designed an articulated locomotive to exploit his system of compounding (bottom); the Baltimore & Ohio Railroad adopted the design in 1904, since when the world's largest steam locomotive has always been a Mallet. This one was built for the Virginian Railway in 1913.

Mary Evans

Union Pacific

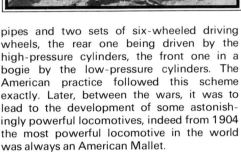

pipes and two sets of six-wheeled driving wheels, the rear one being driven by the high-pressure cylinders, the front one in a bogie by the low-pressure cylinders. The American practice followed this scheme exactly. Later, between the wars, it was to lead to the development of some astonishingly powerful locomotives, indeed from 1904 the most powerful locomotive in the world was always an American Mallet.

As boilers grew longer and taller, drivers found themselves restricted to a side view of the way ahead and under some conditions their vision could easily be obscured by steam. Some lines attempted to overcome this difficulty by separating the two partners in a locomotive crew. The fireman remained on the rear footplate while the driver was placed in a special cab — the locomotives were soon nicknamed 'camelbacks' — halfway along the boiler. This innovation proved unsatisfactory and did not long survive because it restricted communication.

The story of American locomotive design at this period would not be complete without mention of Samuel Matthews Vauclain, who, after serving his apprenticeship with the Pennsylvania Railroad, joined the great Baldwin firm and rose from shop foreman to run the company.

The 'complete railwayman'

As Oswald Nock comments in his book *Railways Then and Now*, Vauclain's career, during which he was directly connected "with the construction of more than 60 000 locomotives, is one of the greatest success stories of the entire railway world; but he was equally a success as an engine designer, a production expert, an administrator, and above all as a businessman who by participating directly in every facet of the job of designing and building locomotives was able to keep his company in the forefront of the trade.

"He retired from the office of president in 1929, and continued as chairman of the board until his death in 1940. As an engine designer he will always be remembered by his ingenious solution to the problem of having a four-cylinder compound with all cylinders outside the frames, to provide that accessibility that was such a cherished precept of American locomotive practice."

The tradition of naming trains is older than most of the railroads in America. In 1847, a service between Boston and a neighbouring seaport was known as the *Steamboat Express,* and there were eventually more than 700 named trains.

In their celebrated *Statistical Account of all the Express Trains of the World* (1889), Foxwell and Farrer found wide divergences of speed in different parts of the United States and few trains which met their minimum standard for an express of an average speed of 40mph, including stops. They reported:

". . . there are a very large number of trains in the Eastern states at 38-39mph, which are most creditable, and in the Western states there are vast quantities of runs at 35-38mph, which are really marvellous performances considering the state of the track (generally single) and the sparse population . . . But it would be almost impossible for any foreigner to do justice to these, and we have had to be content with just top performances . . ."

The fastest running they could find was between Baltimore and Washington, where two trains daily covered the 40 miles in 45 minutes, an average of $53\frac{1}{3}$mph. They also had praise for the long-distance New York-Chicago trains of the Pennsylvania Railroad and New York Central, and also for the times between New York and Philadelphia where there were "26 expresses by the Pennsylvania averaging 42mph and . . . 14 by the Bound Brook route averaging $41\frac{1}{2}$mph.

"(But) many lines where we should expect to find good speeds run no technical 'expresses'; for example, the New York, Lake Erie & Western on its *Chicago and St Louis Limited* takes $12\frac{3}{4}$ hours from Jersey City to Buffalo, 422 miles, speed inclusive only 31mph.

"Again, great as is the reputation of the Boston & Albany, we have to be very indulgent to find an 'express' at all; there is none between the two terminal points, Boston and Albany, and only one (one way) between Worcester and Springfield.

"It must, however, not be forgotten that the entrance to many American towns has to be traversed at very low speeds as the railways are unfenced, running indeed in many cases along the public roads, while intermediate speed has often to be reduced where a railway is crossed on the level, so that the

running speeds may be first-rate, although the 'throughout' speeds *look* poor on paper . . ."

They could find little of note in the West although 'quite first-rate' is the description they applied to the Union Pacific's *Overland Flyer:* "It does the 1031 miles from Omaha (1000 feet above sea level) to Ogden (4301 feet) over two summits of 8427 and 7395 feet (sinking to 6007 feet between) at 29mph inclusive, and $31\frac{1}{4}$ exclusive, of stops".

This, they pointed out, would deserve 'a laurel crown' on the Continent of Europe. "Another admirable run in the Western states," they went on, "is that of the Denver to Rio Grande, narrow gauge, through 771 miles of mountains and gorges at 23mph inclusive from Denver to Ogden; a better performance than the broad gauge Northern Pacific, which does the 1699 miles from St Paul to Wallula, allowing for two hours difference of time, at $26\frac{1}{2}$mph.

"Any of these runs seems to show the energy of these wild Western roads as compared to the slowness of Continental Europe, for even this last train runs quicker by one mile an hour than the Berlin-London express . . ."

Slowest in the world

It was, somewhat predictably, in the Deep South that they found a company, the Scotland Neck Br. W. & W. Railroad, which they thought might "aspire to the proud position of the slowest in the civilized world (excluding, perhaps, Würtemberg)". The scheduled timing on the company's 27-mile route between Weldon and Scotland Neck was 3hr 35min, an average speed of just seven miles an hour.

The early initiative for faster trains was taken in the East. One of the first of the great expresses there was the *New England Limited*, inaugurated in 1891, which ran between Boston and New York. The scheduled time of six hours for a journey of slightly less than 230 miles would not have unduly impressed Foxwell and Farrer.

Nevertheless, the *New England Limited* a magnificently appointed train, made up of Pullman parlour cars, passenger coaches and 'royal buffet' smokers, plus a dining car for the portion of the route between Boston and Willimantic, Conn.

Ronan Picture Library

Pennsylvania Railroad and the Royal Blue line, an amalgamation of three earlier companies. The PR's *Congressional Limited Express* dated from 1895 and the Royal Blue service from 1890, running from the start at more than 45mph.

In 1898 both companies invested in new Pullman stock for these crack trains. On a visit to the Pullman works, a PR executive was smitten by the Brewster green-cream-and-red livery of some private coaches being built for Don Porfirio Diaz, the president of Mexico. The redesigned *Congressional* therefore made its debut under the Mexican national colours. The livery chosen for the new *Royal Limited* were less jazzy — deep blue with gold lettering — but the two dining cars were named 'Waldorf' and 'Astoria' after the two newly-completed New York hotels considered the last word in luxury.

Samuel M. Vauclain (far left), the eminent engineer who became the chairman of the Baldwin Locomotive Works. He is best remembered for his compound locomotive designs.
The interior of a Pullman parlor car with its ornate decorations, elaborate lights, heavy curtains and cane chairs must have reminded many Victorian travellers of home; this scene is from about 1890.
The scene at Philadelphia station, also from about 1890, shows how important it was to have high, airy station roofs in the days of steam locomotives.

Outside, the coaches were white with gold lettering. Inside, the parlour cars and smokers had carpets of thick velvet, white silk curtains and revolving chairs whose plush seats matched the colour of the lettering outside.

White is not, of course, the most practical colour for a train hauled by steam locomotives and the service came to a halt in 1895 when the New York & New England Railroad, which operated the service in conjunction with the New York, New Haven & Hartford Railroad, decided that maintaining the virginal exterior of the coaches was not worth the trouble.

Charles S. Mellon, who became president of the New Haven line in 1903, quickly inaugurated a train which cut an hour off the Boston-New York run and was — inside at least — even more splendid than the *New England Limited* had been.

Its features included private staterooms, observation cars with leather club seats, and a staff of porters and maids to wait upon travellers in the parlour cars. The train was called the *Merchants' Limited*, and the large number of bankers and stockbrokers who used it were kept abreast of the latest news and stockmarket prices by bulletins posted in the observation cars, which doubled as gentlemen's smokers. .

The *Merchants' Limited* was also equipped with two dining cars, one offering an *à la carte* menu, the other a *table d'hôte* menu. The latter featured an elaborate seven-course meal for only a dollar, including grapefruit, soup, baked shad, roast ribs of beef, duckling with current jelly, roast short ribs with brown potatoes, vegetables, salads, dessert, cakes, cheese and coffee. The menu was backed up by an excellent wine list.

Initially, through coaches bound from Boston to New York and points south faced a two-hour ferry journey from the Harlem River, north of New York, down the East River to Jersey City, where locomotives of the Pennsylvania Railroad took over. It was not actually until 1917, with completion of the giant Hell Gate Bridge, that there was a through all-*rail* route from Boston to the South.

By then, a tradition of competition with *de luxe* trains over the New York-Philadelphia-Baltimore-Washington route had existed for well over a quarter of a century between the

Ronan Picture Library

The rivalry of these two great trains was to last for 60 years.

The playground for rich Americans in the last quarter of the nineteenth century was the French Riviera. Henry Morrison Flagler, a founder of Standard Oil, decided that Florida could be a competitor for this exclusive winter holiday trade, given the right facilities and comfortable means of reaching them.

At St Augustine he built an ornate hotel whose decor was inspired by the Alhambra Palace in Granada (Spain) and, from Pullman, he ordered the *Florida Special,* a train which had bellows connections between every coach, electric lighting, and, as one observer recorded, a crew decked out in uniforms which were 'so gaudy and gorgeous' that they looked like Prussian officers.

The *Florida Special,* which made its inaugural run in January 1888, was followed by the rival *Seaboard Florida Limited* in 1903.

With Florida and the Caribbean starting to boom, the original Flagler line was extended in 1912 across the numerous islands to Key West where passengers could catch a steamer bound for Havana, Cuba, 90 miles away. Thirty-three years later, this unique route was wrecked by a hurricane and eventually replaced by a road.

It was the journey between two important cities, London and Edinburgh, that inspired the great railway races in Britain. Similarly, it was rivalry between the New York Central and the Pennsylvania Railroad for passenger traffic between New York and Chicago that led to the creation of one of the most prestigious of all American trains, the *Twentieth Century Limited.*

Until 1893 both the PR and the NYC offered a 24-hour service between New York and Chicago. In that year, however, a great international exhibition was held in Chicago. George H. Daniels, the NYC's passenger agent who had learned a few showman's tricks during an earlier career as a salesman for patent medicines, took the opportunity to inaugurate the *Exposition Flyer,* booked to cut four hours off the journey and achieve the creditable average speed of 49mph.

The *Exposition Flyer* took the Lake Shore route (along the shore of Lake Erie). Its PR rival – the *Pennsylvania Limited,* which entered service for the first time in 1887 and had the distinction of being the first train in the world to be equipped with bellows connections throughout – followed a slightly shorter, but steeper, route. At this stage, however, the PR declined the challenge to make a race of it.

The decision was a wise one. The NYC found it difficult to run the *Exposition Flyer* to time, and withdrew the train when the

exhibition ended, reverting to the old 24-hour schedule. But Daniels was not a man to give up easily and, in 1897, he inaugurated a daily 20-hour service, using luxury Wagner cars (a rival to Pullman's). The new train, the *Lake Shore Limited*, sparked off a speed-with-service 'war' between the NYC and the PR which was to last nearly half a century.

Its main features are graphically captured by Arthur D. Dubin in his contribution to the book *The Great Trains*. Each of the three rakes of the *Lake Shore Limited* "comprised seven of the most sumptuous cars ever built for public service. The entire train sparkled in its light olive lined with gold; and this inevitably provoked a rejoinder, so that two months later the Pennsylvania company inaugurated one of the most colourful trains ever operated in the United States – the *New Pennsylvania Limited*, resplendent in a Brewster-green and cream livery and trimmed with so much gold leaf that the irreverent referred to it as the 'Yellow Kid'.

'Centuries' and 'Specials'

"The NYC's reply, made four years later, was . . . the *Twentieth Century Limited*. But on the same day in 1902 as this entered service the rival countered with its *Pennsylvania Special*. Like the railway races from London to Scotland, the NYC *versus* Pennsy war was reported throughout the newspaper world – though it should be noted that there was at first no attempt at clipping speeds and the battle was rather to keep to 45 or 50mph schedules over indifferent tracks . . .

"The first *Century* of 1902 was composed of both Pullman- and railroad-owned cars. The diners were 'attractively finished in Santiago mahogany . . . all linen, silverware and crockery were manufactured to order.' The buffet was equipped with club facilities which included a barber's shop, a bath and a smoking room. Similar equipment was to be found on the Pennsylvania trains.

"When the Pennsy reduced its running time to 18 hours in 1905, a speed war at last flared up . . . The *Pennsylvania Special* was then soon advertised as 'the fastest long-distance train in the world' – and this was despite an early set-back, for on its maiden trip, westbound, the *Special* had developed a hot box and lost valuable time.

"After entering the system's western division 26 minutes behind schedule the engineer, piloting a borrowed freight locomotive, is reported to have covered more than 131 miles in 115 minutes and to have speeded over a three-mile stretch at above 127mph. Needless to say . . . these figures have been challenged by many experts, and certainly the second claim seems wholly incredible. But undoubtedly some very fine performances were put up.

"For many years the rivalry of these two great lines continued, with every improvement on one being matched by the other. In 1912, for instance, the *Century* too was advertised as 'the fastest long-distance train in the world: 960 miles in 18 hours', and its new amenities included fresh and salt water baths, manicure service and a stenographer . . ."

Opposite, top: A beautifully fitted parlor car built by one of the Pullman's rivals, the Wagner North Shore Sleeping Car Company.
Henry M. Flagler (left) was one of the founders of the Standard Oil Company and a noted hotelier; one of his most famous luxury hotels was the Ponce de Leon at St Augustine in Florida, seen opposite (below).
Vestibule connections between cars were a fresh innovation in the 1890s and were adopted by all luxury trains (below).
Bottom: A dining car on the Chicago, Burlington & Quincy Railroad in about 1890.

Burlington Northern

Western Americana

Chicago, one of the focal points of this long-running battle, was already the world's greatest railway centre by the last decade of the century. Main lines belonging to no fewer than 22 companies ran north, south, east and west from 'The Windy City', and the giant Union Stock Yards alone handled 12 million sheep, pigs and head of cattle a year.

Although Chicago eventually had six main line termini, it was not until 1946 that there were through-carriage facilities between the eastern and western halves of the city. Until then, passengers frequently had to face the inconvenience of not only changing trains, but stations, and having to wait a long time for their connection.

The ultimate train

Foxwell and Farrer made the comment in their 1889 book that the journey through the United States from the Atlantic to the Pacific was spoiled "by the extraordinary badness of the connections in Chicago (wait 10½ hours)".

Freight was better catered for. In 1882, 13 of the companies serving the city joined forces to create the Belt Railroad Co., which ultimately had 22 miles of east-west

track, plus 300 miles of sidings and marshalling yards. At the peak of its operations, the Belt needed 75 steam locomotives to handle the movement of 6000 freight wagons a day.

There has never been a truly transcontinental train in the United States and to travel between the two great oceans on either side of the country has always meant changing at some inland city like Chicago. Nevertheless, the frontier tradition ensured that the expresses which plied across what had once been the Wild West had a glamour peculiarly their own.

In the Deep South there was the *Sunset Limited*, which went into service in 1894, making the 2500-mile trip between New Orleans and San Francisco in 75 hours, "the shortest possible limit consistent with safety", an average speed of 33mph. The original *Sunset* matched the splendour of the east coast expresses. It had a library and bathroom, and its dining car, called the Epicure, served "viands peculiar to the land and climate traversed". The *Sunset* proved so popular that the service was progressively increased until it became daily in 1913.

From 1911 to 1918, one of the finest trains the world has ever known, in terms of comfort, service and cuisine, ran from Dodge

City, Kansas, to Los Angeles through the deserts of Arizona and New Mexico. It was named the *Santa Fe de Luxe* because it ran over the Atchison, Topeka & Sante Fe line following the old, lawless Sante Fe trail. Even the *Chief* and *Super Chief* of later years could not match the luxury of the *Santa Fe de Luxe*.

North Pacific's magnate

Farther north, the Northern Pacific inaugurated the *North Coast Limited* in 1900, covering the 2000 miles between St Paul and Seattle in 62½ hours. It was one of the first trains to be equipped with an observation-lounge car so that passengers could obtain maximum enjoyment from the scenery. In 1905 the Northern Pacific owner, Jim Hill, realized a long-standing ambition with a new St Paul-Seattle service, the *Oriental Limited*, which connected with his own 20000-ton steamship, the *Minnesota*, plying between Seattle and the Far East. Four years later, in honour of the Seattle World Fair, the *Oriental's* route was extended even farther inland to Chicago.

Hill, who built the Great Northern, completed in 1895, and acquired control of the Northern Pacific soon afterwards, was cast in

Jim Hill, the Great Northern Railway's indomitable entrepreneur (far left).
A track laying machine at work for the Atchison, Topeka & Santa Fe Railway in Oklahoma in 1909 (left).
The North Coast Limited at speed on the Northern Pacific Railway about 1900 (right). The train was replete with all the luxuries of electric light, steam heating, baths and barber and valet service.
The last spike is driven into the track of the Great Northern Railway completing the route from St Paul, Minnesota to Seattle, Washington, in 1893 (below).
The UP used the Pacific type locomotive on express passenger trains. Illustrated (bottom) is a design of 1914, after modifications had been made.

Burlington Northern

the larger-than-life mould of most of America's great railroad pioneers.

Physically he was immensely strong, and, when his office caught fire on one occasion, he saved his records by picking up a rolltop desk weighing 300 pounds and hurling it through a window into the street. Emotionally he could be abrasive or kind, mean or generous. On meeting a new clerk for the first time and learning that his name was Charles Swinburne Spittles, Hill fired him on the spot, snapping: "I don't like your name and I don't like your face."

When a resort complained that his railroad was noisy and a blot on the landscape, Hill showed them who was boss by moving the depot an inconvenient two miles out of town. In the process, he ruined the charter fishing business of a friend, Tom Wise. To compensate him, Hill built a lakeside pavilion, equipped it lavishly with fishing tackle and a fleet of 20 boats, and then handed the whole concern over to Wise without charging him a cent.

The Great Northern differed from the other Pacific routes in that it was built when the policy of generous government land grants and subsidies had ceased. Hence, to save money, much greater attention had to

Western Americana

be paid to sound engineering principles than had been the case with the earlier lines.

Keith Wheeler recalls in *The Railroaders*, part of the *Time-Life* series on *The Old West*: ''To bring the line over the Rockies, he found a 36-year-old engineer named John F. Stevens, who had made an enviable reputation in planning the tortuous route of the Denver & Rio Grande narrow-gauge railroad.

''Far out in Montana, Hill set Stevens to the task of rediscovering the 'lost' Marias River Pass, which Meriwether Lewis had originally heard about from Indians in 1805, but had been unable to locate.

''Travelling afoot with one Flathead Indian guide (who gave out in the dead of winter), Stevens finally found the gateway in 1889. In time, it lifted the Great Northern over the spine of the country at 5200 feet on a grade of one per cent.''

To ensure that his boxcars were kept full, Hill built branch lines every few miles to tap the resources of the surrounding countryside. He also increased these resources by interesting rich friends in the exploitation of the vast new acres of virgin countryside.

$53m. millionaire

It was on Hill's initiative that Junius Beebe of Boston planted a sprawling apple ranch in Washington which eventually needed four and a half miles of GN freightcars to ship the annual crop. Hill also introduced lumber king Frederick Weyerhaeuser to the Northwest, a step that led to the creation of today's vast lumber industry.

His one great error was to believe that the rolling Montana uplands could be made to produce billions of tons of wheat. A combination of deep-ploughing techniques and

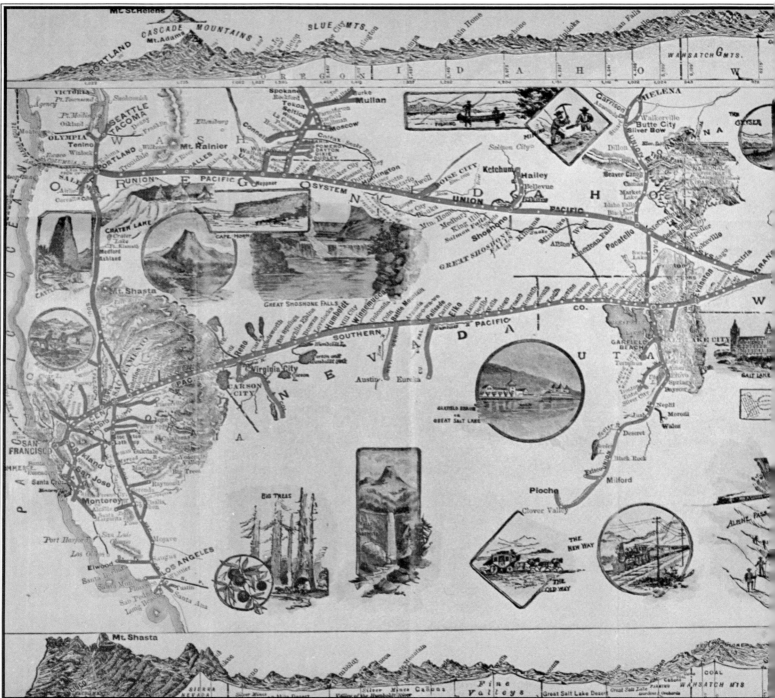

lack of rain produced the first of the great dust bowls in the West.

Hill — known variously as 'Little Giant', 'Empire Builder' and 'One-Eyed Old Sonofabitch' (he was blind in one eye as a result of a childhood accident) — eventually presided over a railroad empire that stretched from Canada in the north to Missouri in the south, from the Great Lakes to Puget Sound on the Pacific, and from there to the Orient via his own steamship line.

When he died at the age of 78, he left a fortune of 53 million dollars and a reputation, despite his personal quirks, as a visionary who had benifited his country.

The last two transcontinental lines in the United States were the Chicago, Milwaukee & St Paul of 1909 and the Western Pacific, completed between Salt Lake City and Oakland in 1910. The former's *de luxe* expresses,

The Columbian and *The Olympian*, covered the 2200 miles between Chicago and the West Coast in three days and the company described them as 'fit for the gods'.

Inadequate signals

By this time, Britain had a highly sophisticated signalling system. All signals and points on lines used by passenger trains were interlocked, and, between stations, drivers stopped or proceeded according to the set of the signals.

Up to the 1920s, however, U.S. railroads had an unsatisfactory accident record, not only in interlocked and automatically-signalled areas but on the thousands of miles of track where there were no signals at all and drivers had to proceed in accordance with written orders, which might be faulty or could be misunderstood.

John F. Stevens, the brilliant engineer who not only built the narrow-gauge Denver & Rio Grande route through Colorado, but also built the Great Northern Railway through the mountains of the north-western United States (far left).
Tourist map of Union Pacific lines and connecting lines, 1893 (below).

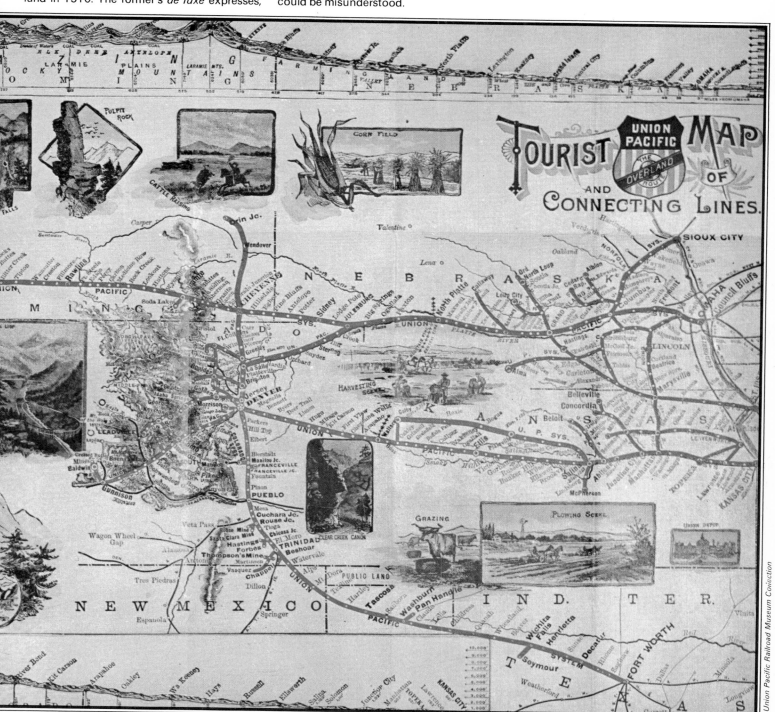

One spectacular accident — for reasons never clearly established — involved no less famous a train than the *Twentieth Century Limited* during a run from New York to Chicago in 1905. In some mysterious way, points at Mentor, on the shores of Lake Erie, which had been correctly set at one time, were interfered with.

As a result, the express travelling at 60mph was switched without warning into a siding and, still at full speed, crashed into a freight shed where the leading coaches burst into flames, causing a heavy death toll.

North of the 49th parallel, the Canadian Pacific had inaugurated its first transcontinental service on June 28, 1886 when a 12-coach train — including two sleeping cars equipped with bathrooms — set out from Montreal on the six-day journey to Port Moody, British Colombia.

The CP's luxury transcontinental express, the *Imperial Limited*, made its first run from Montreal to Vancouver in 1899, covering the 2900 miles in 100 hours. It was, however, a train of contrasts. The luxury coaches, built of red Honduras mahogany, had Louis XV interiors, finished in ivory and gold. But the train also hauled a colonist car, with primitive cooking and sleeping accommodation (no bedding, for example), to provide cheap fares for European settlers on their way to new homes in under-populated outposts of the country.

The success of the Canadian Pacific led eventually to an extraordinary situation in which no fewer than three companies were building transcontinental routes across the country without very much concern either for cost or whether they would pay their way.

Canadian contenders

The Grand Trunk Pacific proposed to link its existing eastern interests with a route via Winnipeg, Saskatoon, Edmonton, Jasper and then through the wilds of British Columbia to Prince Rupert on the coast. The Canadian Northern envisaged running virtually parallel with the GTP as far as Jasper, then dropping south to Kamloops and running alongside the Canadian Pacific into Vancouver.

The third contender, put forward in 1903, was the National Transcontinental Railway, which would start at Moncton, New Brunswick, cross the St Lawrence River at Quebec and make a beeline for Winnipeg in the centre of the country.

The government encouraged all three schemes, hoping among other things that they would stimulate settlement, but despite official aid the three companies found themselves in financial difficulties by the time the First World War broke out and had to be taken under federal control. When the war ended, they were nationalized as the Canadian National Railways.

Left: Canadian Pacific poster (1893) advertising tours at home and abroad. Opposite: An early passenger train into Edmonton in 1905 (top), Pullman drawing room car on the 'International Limited', famous Canadian express (centre), and a pioneer train of the Grand Trunk Pacific Railway heading west out of Winnipeg in 1908 (bottom).

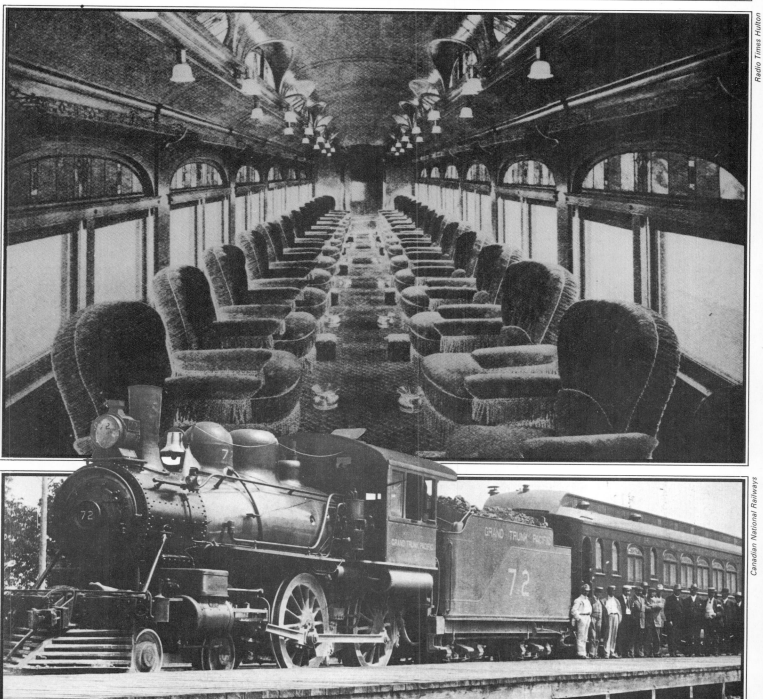

THE CHANGING FACE

In 1850, a quarter of a century after Stephenson had first demonstrated the power of the locomotive over the Stockton-Darlington line, the United States topped the railway league with 9072 miles of track. Next came Britain (6658) followed by Germany (3777) and France (1927). Spain had only 17 miles, Switzerland 16, South America 16, Sweden and Mexico 7 each. Africa, Asia and Australia had none at all.

The next 40 years saw a dramatic extension and, by 1890, the basis of modern railway networks had been laid, or planned, nearly everywhere in the world.

Iberia and Scandinavia

Government indecision delayed the coming of the railroad in Spain and it was not until 1848 that the first train went into service between Barcelona and Mataró. A royal commission on the question of gauge settled, despite contrary advice from the ageing George Stephenson, on two Spanish yards (1674mm). The obvious economic benefits lay in linking Spain with the rest of Europe. In 1856 work began on the difficult 400-mile mountainous route between Valladolid, to the north of Madrid, and Irún on the Biscay frontier with France.

In the same year, Portugal's first railway, between Lisbon and Corregado, was opened by King Pedro V. In order to avoid isolation from the remainder of Europe, Portugal was virtually committed to adopting the same gauge as Spain although they made the gesture of choosing two Portuguese yards (1665mm). In terms of railway operation, the difference of nine mm is too small to be of any practical importance. Both gauges are very near 5ft 6in (1676mm) and the Iberian peninsula remains 5ft 6in territory to this day.

The first railway in Denmark was the Baltic Line, a 91-mile stretch of track from Altona to Kiel, which opened in September 1844. Despite the appropriation of this line in 1866 by Germany and the physical disadvantages posed by the fact that the country consists of a peninsula and a number of scattered islands, Denmark went on to build a comprehensive rail system.

In Norway it was the mountains which presented the main impediment. A short stretch of the line which now connects Oslo (Christiana, as it was then called) with

OF THE WORLD

Trondheim to the north, was opened in 1854 but not completed until after the First World War, while the other main lines from Oslo — to Bergen, Stavanger, Stockholm and Copenhagen — progressed almost as slowly.

Plans for a national railway system were drawn up early in Sweden where, in the southern part of the country at least, the terrain is less formidable. It was decided that the state would build the main trunk routes with the feeder lines being left to private enterprise, a pattern for development which was to persist for a century. The first state route, between Malmö and Lund in the southern tip of the country, went into service in 1856 and the first private line opened the same year.

Russia's first railroad, completed late in 1836, was 17 miles long and connected the capital, St Petersburg (now Leningrad),

Mansell

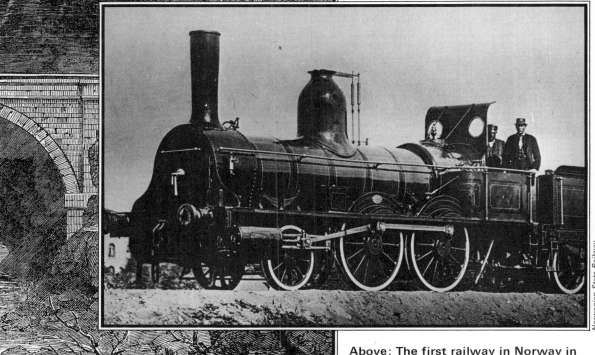

Norwegian State Railway

Above: The first railway in Norway in 1854 had this neat locomotive built by Robert Stephenson & Company.
The Techas Pass (left) takes the Bilbao-Tudela Railway through a difficult, mountainous route in Spain, 1863.

with the pleasure palace of Czar Nicolas I. The track, with a gauge of 6ft, was laid on top of an embankment to prevent drifting snow from interfering with the service. Initially, horses provided the motive power unless there were more than 50 passengers. The horses were then replaced by a locomotive which, on the orders of the Czar, had been fitted with a spectacular warning device made up of 11 horns and a trombone.

Rule of the sword

Shortly afterwards, the American engineer George Washington Whistler, who had built the Boston & Worcester (first section opened in 1835), arrived to construct the St Petersburg-Moscow Railway. Whistler chose a gauge of 5ft (1524mm), which remains the gauge of today's vast Soviet network. The story goes that the Czar, probably tiring of

discussions about terrain and possible difficulties with landowners, slammed his sword down on a map and used it to draw a straight line between the two cities, saying: "That will be the route of your railway." In the event, the railway was not built quite like that: the 125mph trains which the Soviet Union started to run in 1976 have to slow down in a number of places because of the curvature of the track.

Lines followed to Warsaw and from Moscow to Kiev and Sebastopol. Others connected the Black Sea and the Caspian and stretched out towards the east. The tracks were, in general, poorly laid and train schedules correspondingly slow. In the mid-1860s, Russia's finest express was expected to cover the 403 miles between St Petersburg and Moscow at an average speed of 21mph and did not always succeed in keep-

In Sweden the state built the main trunk routes, leaving the feeder lines to private enterprise. In the station at Torboda (below) is a British-built 1856 locomotive designed by Bayer Peacock. The first Russian railway track linked the palace of Czar Nicolas I with his capital, St Petersburg (now Leningrad). By 1864 the Imperial Russian Railway was extremely luxurious, as scenes on the Odessa to Kiev train (right) show. The restaurant car (top left); the kitchen (top right) is the earliest example recorded of cooking facilities on trains. The second-class carriage and washroom (centre) are comfortable and carpeted, but pale beside the white upholstery, ornate ceilings and rich carpets of the first-class carriages by day (left) and night (right).

Mary Evans

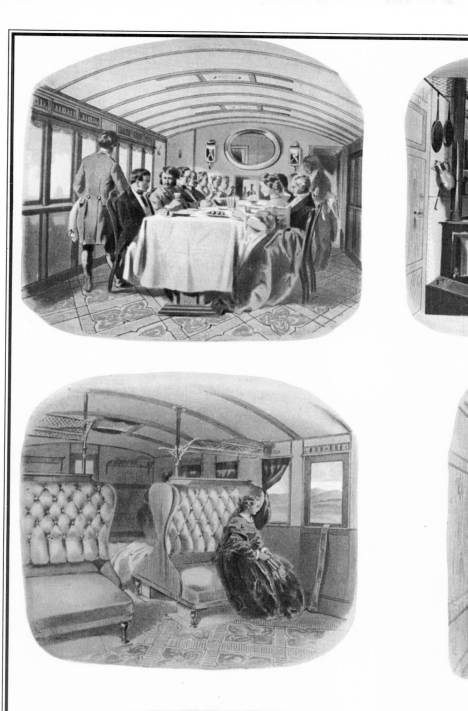

ing to this modest timetable. In 1880 the average speed of the fastest train between the two cities had risen to only 26mph, but this was equal to other European trains of the time, always excepting Britain where 40mph was achieved.

Czar goes off the rails

Czar Alexander II, who succeeded Nicolas, was a railway enthusiast who grasped the value of the railway in maintaining control over his vast kingdom. He bought a 15-coach train which had belonged to Napoleon III and equipped it as lavishly as any of the private coaches belonging to American millionaires. Unfortunately, Alexander decreed that any train on which he was travelling should be driven at maximum speed, an order which, taken in conjunction with the state of Russian tracks, ensured that his career as a

railway traveller was punctuated by derailments. In the most serious of them, 16 court officials were killed.

During the years 1840 to 1890 the British were acquiring or consolidating an empire and railways were found to be a useful tool in the process. India provides a classic example. The first 21-mile track opened between Bombay and Thana in April 1853, but, although a commission had recommended a network of lines covering the country, it took the Indian Mutiny of 1857 to give genuine urgency to the task.

Calcutta was linked with Delhi, 1020 miles away, in 1860 and the 1300-mile Calcutta-Bombay line completed in 1870. By 1880, India had more than nine thousand miles of railway and the total continued to grow, more than quadrupling over the next 20 years. The main routes were built to a

China's first railway (below) got off to a bad start in 1876 – owners of alternative transport protested it would put them out of work and many people were superstitious – the authorities were forced to pull up the track the following year.
The Japanese were more receptive, beginning with the Tokyo-Yokohama line in 1872. By 1880 the railway was steaming through Takanawa, according to this artist's impression (top right). The Burma Railways opened in 1876 with a fleet of 20 small locomotives of the standard metre gauge shown below. In Algeria the first railways were run by the Paris, Lyons & Mediterranean Railway. Coaches (below right) were identical to the main-line coaches in France.

108

gauge of 5ft 6in, but from 1870 feeder lines were constructed to a metre gauge. It meant – and continues to mean – considerable inconvenience in the trans-shipment of goods. On the other hand, it brought the benefits of the railroad to many parts of the country where the terrain would have made the laying of a 5ft 6in track impossibly expensive.

A Frenchman in India

In the 1860s, some of the Indian trains led the world in passenger comfort, having built double-decker first-class coaches which included sleeping accommodation, servants' quarters, lavatories and showers. Louis Rousselet, a French author who undertook a five-and-a-half day rail trip on the East Indian Railway at this time, wrote of his experience: "I travelled over this immense distance with comparatively little fatigue, sleeping at night on a comfortable little bed and walking up and down in my carriage during the day. At stations provided with buffets I found a servant who, when he had taken the orders for my meal, telegraphed it to the next station where my breakfast or dinner awaited my arrival."

Of the sleeping arrangements, he noted: "These carriages contained only two compartments in each of which there is but a single seat, the movable back of which takes off, and being fastened by leather straps forms a sort of couch of the same description as the beds in ships' cabins. On the opposite side of the carriage are two closets – one for the toilet and the other the convenience. By paying a slight addition to the price of the ordinary fare, you might travel thus surrounded by all the comforts so essential in this country."

It is perhaps worth making the comment that another 60 years were to pass before even a royal train in Britain was equipped with a bath.

Stop-go in China

In China, railway construction was hotly opposed, partly on superstitious grounds, partly on economic. The bearers of sedan chairs and the owners of junks and sampans argued that the railway would put them out of business. Attempts by foreign commercial interests to build a railway in Peking in 1863 and in the dock area of Shanghai in 1875 had to be abandoned because of the violent demonstrations against them.

A further barrier existed in the form of provincial rulers who, like the German states, feared that a through railway route would rob them of the customs dues they

exacted. The only way around these impediments was imperial decree. At the time, Emperor Kuang Hsü was still a child and effective power lay in the hands of his mother, the Empress. It is said that the forward-looking statesman Li Hung-chang eventually won both of them over to the cause of the railway by making the child Emperor a present of a clockwork train set. By 1890, however, China still had only 125 miles of track.

Japan chooses British

Japan, in contrast, was much more receptive to Western ideas. British engineers built the country's first railway, a 17-mile line between Tokyo and Yokohama which opened in 1872, and gave it the 3ft 6in gauge which is still retained by Japanese National Railways today. From this point railway construction continued steadily and became a fundamental element in the emergence of Japan as a giant industrial power.

It is interesting that India should have chosen a metre rather than 3ft 6in (1067mm) for its feeder lines. The decision can be traced to the influence of Lord Dalhousie, governor-general in the late 1840s, who was an early campaigner in favour of Britain going metric. In future years, British engineers based in India were to carry this metre gauge round the Indian Ocean to Kenya, Uganda, Aden, Iraq, Burma, Malaya (which in turn influenced Siam to adopt metre gauge) and North Borneo.

Elsewhere in southern Africa, because of South African influence, gauges tended to be 3ft 6in. The first railway in South Africa was a short standard gauge line from Durban to Point, opened in 1860, and it was followed by a similar railway out of Cape Town in 1863. By government decision the Cape Town line was altered to 3ft 6in during 1875. This led to the use of 3ft 6in gauge later in Rhodesia, Zambia, Malawi and Mozambique, as well as extensively in Angola and Zaïre, for by the time all these came to be built the international nature of railways was clearly recognized.

British rail travels

Sudan had a 3ft 6in line in 1875, and, in addition to Japan, British engineers took the gauge to Ecuador, Central America, Newfoundland, Dutch Java, Sumatra and, surprisingly, even to Norway for some of the country's minor lines.

The discovery of diamonds was a basic factor in the building of the South African line north to Kimberley and on to Mafeking,

Popper

and mining of one sort or another was the spur to railway construction in all the continents. Often these mine railways were of considerable length and, as a secondary matter, served to open up the countries in which they were built. Such were the Antofagasta Railway of 1888 in northern Chile, later extended to give Bolivia a railway outlet to the sea, and the Imperial Brazilian Colliery Railway of 1886. Iron ore similarly led a French company to build the line between Mokta el Hadid and the port of Bône (now Annaba) in Algeria as early as 1864.

Gauge down under

Queensland in Australia had its first line, from Ipswich to Grandchester, in 1865, selecting a 3ft 6in gauge as the most economical and practical. In 1871, 3ft 6in was used in Tasmania, and later in Western Australia. As these three states are as far apart as it is possible to get in Australia — Tasmania is an island, anyway — and the intervening areas use either 5ft 3in or standard gauge, the various states have been accused of being individualistic in railway construction with no interest in working together. It seems more probable that the states were dependent on the advice of their engineers and this confusion of gauges has arisen because railway engineering ideas were in their infancy during the construction period.

However, they worked to the benefit of neighbouring New Zealand where the first railway, opened in 1869, was a short length of 5ft 3in track from Christchurch to Ferrymead. By government decision in 1870, all the railways in the country were to be altered to, or built to, the 3ft 6in gauge. The lack of a common policy in Australia meant that New Zealand was able to sell its 5ft 3in-gauge locomotives to South Australia.

The one-minute mile

By 1890, railways had been so much improved that they served their countries well, offering to carry all types of traffic at a reasonable speed and with safety. Most British main lines and some eastern United States railroads could offer express passenger trains that averaged more than 40mph, including stops, and trains could reach over 70mph at some point in their journeys. In other European countries, average speeds, including stops, rarely exceeded 30mph. Nevertheless, for passengers and freight, this was rapid by the standards of the day. The railway had come a long way in 65 years and changed the face, and the habits, of the world.

India Office Library

The São Paulo Railway Company, Brazil, built four rope-worked inclines to get up the coastal mountain range from Port Santos, (far left).
The rack railway up the Corcovado mountain in Rio, opened in 1884, first used Swiss locomotives, which were joined in 1886 by two solid American ones (below left).
The Indian Railways system had not only luxurious service, but (left) magnificent stations. Axel Haig's Bombay Station, built in the late 1870s, still stands.
The Fairlie locomotive 'Snake' (below) was built for the New Zealand Railways in 1874; it is an improved version of an articulated double-ender built in 1851 for the Semmering trials.

New Zealand Railways

RAILWAYS ROUND THE

In terms of difficult terrain and appalling working conditions, some of the greatest challenges still lay ahead of railway builders in 1890. For Russia, the most pressing need was to open up the vast wastes beyond the Ural Mountains.

By the last decade of the century the country's main lines formed a cross with Moscow at its centre and the routes ran north to St Petersburg (now Leningrad), south to the ice-free naval and commercial port of Odessa on the Black Sea, west to Warsaw and east to Nizhni Novgorod (now Gorki), scene of Europe's biggest horse fair.

No train in Russia had a name. No fast train carried third-class passengers and many of the first-class seats were reserved for holders of priority tickets. The word 'fast' was, furthermore, strictly relative. In 1889, date of the celebrated Foxwell-Farrer survey, only one Russian train qualified — and then only by the flimsiest of margins — as an express according to their 29mph yardstick.

The first named train finally appeared in 1894. It was the *Courier*, which covered the 405 miles between Kiev and Odessa at an average speed of 34mph and, on one section, an unheard-of 40mph. As the name implies, this night express was largely for the use of naval officers and government officials; private citizens, however well-endowed or well-connected, had little hope of boarding it.

By this time, Russia had begun to look to its Wild East as, half a century earlier, the United States had looked to its Wild West. Beyond the Urals lay rich farmland that could become the country's granary. Farther east again lay Siberia, hostile in climate, barely populated, but rich in minerals. And beyond Siberia lay Japan, hostile in a different sense, against whom it seemed fairly certain that Russia would one day have to fight a war.

In the construction of the Trans-Siberian railway 15 million sleepers were used, sufficient for over 6000 miles of single track. Insert: War propaganda illustration of Japanese troops firing on a hospital train during the Russo-Japanese war (1904–05). Children selling flowers at a wayside station on the Trans-Siberian railway, 1913 (top right).

Mary Evans

WORLD

Out of this combination of economic and military needs, plus the broader interest of political unity, was born one of the greatest of all railway concepts, greater than anything in the New World – the Trans-Siberian Railway, stretching nearly 5000 miles from the Urals to the ice-free port of Vladivostok on the Pacific.

It was not uncommon at the time for travellers to take two years over this journey. A start on building the railway, which would cut the time (at least on paper) to two weeks, was made at Vladivostok in 1891. Nicolas, heir to the Czar, was present in person to give the project a formal initiation and provide living proof of uneasy Russo-Japanese relations. On his head was a freshly-healed scar from an assassination attempt with a Samurai sword.

Work began at the other end of the route the following year. Thousands of convicts and exiles worked on the line in conditions as harsh, and often harsher, than those encountered anywhere else in the world where men have built railways. In the empty heart of Siberia, there were places where the temperature rose above zero for only two months of the year and sank to minus 47°C (−50°F) in mid-winter.

Nevertheless, with the track lightly-laid and few earthworks, progress was rapid, and, by 1900, the Baltic was linked to the Pacific by an almost continuous railway route across Russia. A great natural barrier still remained in Lake Baikal, one of the biggest freshwater lakes in the world, and the deepest.

Until the line was completed through the difficult mountain territory around the southern shore of the lake, passengers had to leave their train at Irkutsk – still more than 2000 miles from their destination – and cross to Tanchoi on the eastern shore by a ferry steamer, prefabricated in England by Armstrong-Whitworth and shipped out to Russia for assembly.

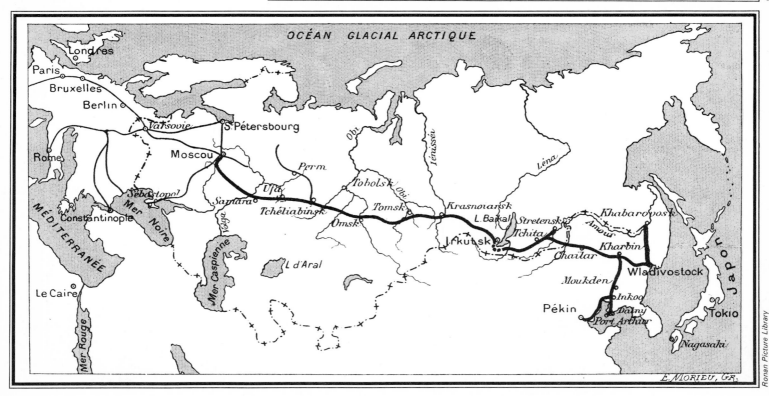

The ferry could not operate in winter, when Lake Baikal froze to a depth of ten feet. This difficulty was overcome initially by dogs and sleds and then by laying 25 miles of temporary track across the surface of the lake once the ice was five feet deep.

From 1900 there was a regular service to Vladivostok, but as K. Westcott Jones points out in his contribution to *The Great Trains*, it was "the railway-minded British" who "christened the train the *Trans-Siberian Express* after the Russians had announced the start of a public service: for the completion of the line was a matter of great importance for British travellers to the Far East and indeed to the Foreign Office in London.

"French and German diplomats, too, realised that they were going to use it. All at once, the journey to an embassy in Peking or Tokyo was cut from six to seven weeks to barely a fortnight — if all went well. The service had an impact on long-distance travellers akin to that of flying boats 30 years later, and the powerful P&O shipping line became seriously worried by it."

Two trains made the journey each week, the *International Express*, made up of *Wagons-Lits* coaches, and the *State Express*, made up of Russian rolling stock. On the journey, scheduled to last two weeks, *Wagons-Lits* provided a bath coach, a gymnasium and a lounge complete with piano.

Opposite, top: A saloon coach on the Trans-Siberian railway (1900), with piano for the entertainment of passengers.
Convicts engaged on the construction of the railway near Nertchinsk (centre).
Below: A French map of about 1904 showing the original route. The later proposed route around Lake Baikal is shown by a dotted line.

Above: Passengers on the Trans-Siberian railway were aboard for several days; to keep fit the energetic could make use of this travelling gymnasium. Below: The pre-1914 Trans-Siberian Express in all its imposing glory.

However, experienced travellers usually allowed an extra week for the trip. The lightly-laid track and the severity of the Russian winter, followed by destructive spring thaws, were responsible for an average of two derailments and long delays on each trip, and even when they were not victims of such mishaps the two so-called expresses rarely managed to average more than a limping 15mph.

The outbreak of the Russo-Japanese War in February 1904, meant a temporary end to the *Trans-Siberian Express* due to the demands of the army. Russia now began to feel the full impact of the inadequacies of the track and the failure, even at this late date, to complete the route around the south of Lake Baikal.

Only three trains a day could be worked over the single-track line and they rarely managed more than five mph. Between Tanchoi and the front, far greater capacity was needed and a herd of a thousand horses had to be assembled to haul 65

locomotives, 25 coaches and more than 2000 wagons across the ice railway.

A crash programme resulted in the 160-mile line around the south of the lake being completed within seven months although at the enormous cost for the period of £52 000 a mile. Altogether, during the 18 months the war lasted, an army of a million men, together with their equipment and munitions, were transported east. In addition to the soldiers and equipment, ambulance trains were sent to the front.

War effort hindered

However, this was not enough. General Kuropatkin of Russia said later: "Wonders were effected – but it was too late." The war may be said to have been lost because of the inadequacies of the railway. When Russia conceded defeat the number of troops she had available outnumbered the Japanese by ten to one, but there was no means of getting them to the front.

Russia recovered quite quickly from this

set-back and the years prior to the First World War saw many improvements to railway services and speeds. The first through service between Berlin and Moscow was inaugurated in 1912 with the two sleeper coaches being lifted into the air at the Polish frontier for conversion to the Russian 5-ft gauge.

Better track enabled the *International Express* to offer a nine-day service between Moscow and Vladivostok with little risk of derailment, more baths than before *and* a coach that contained a library and reading room. Shortly before the First World War came Russia's fastest train, the night express between St Petersburg and Moscow, which averaged just over 40mph, including four stops.

However, the war brought decline in railway performance, followed by the chaos of the October Revolution and civil war. It was not until the 1950s that Russia again had a train as fast as the old St Petersburg-Moscow express.

Hamlyn Group

In Australia, the great challenge was to connect Western Australia with the rest of the country by means of a railway line across the flat, sun-scorched Nullarbor Plain where there were no trees, no water, no people, no animals – nothing but dust and blazing heat.

The onset of the First World War made the matter one of strategic importance. The federal government, which had come into being with creation of the Commonwealth in 1901, put up the money and also made the farsighted decision that the track would be standard gauge, despite the fact that it would link up at Kalgoorlie with the 3ft 6in gauge of Western Australia and at Port Augusta with the 3ft 6in gauge favoured by part of South Australia (elsewhere in the state the gauge was 5ft 3in).

The construction gangs had to take everything with them, including camels as draught animals, and what it was like to work on the project has been graphically described by one ganger:

"I started off on the construction of the east-west line in 1914, shovelling sand for 10s 6d a day on stale bread, oily butter, salt beef and a bit of rice. It was a tough job. I doubt if we will ever again see men work under the conditions the men on the Trans-Australia did with horses, camels, shovels and picks.

"Remember that on this 900 miles not one stream of water was crossed, no man lived and the land was so flat no tunnel had to be built, no bridge across gulches. We lived in tent-houses – sometimes wood part way up with a canvas top, sometimes a cutting in the earth with a tent above that.

"Even as the line was being built we had to use sand scoops fastened on to the front of a slow-moving train to clear the sand off the line. We kept flour, baking powder, pepper and salt on hand in case we were cut off, and, of course, vinegar and onions for turkeys."

Locomotives were ordered from Britain – 4-6-0s for passenger traffic, 2-8-0s for goods – and built by the North British Locomotive Co. of Glasgow. The strategic importance of the line ensured that the order had high priority, despite the many other demands being made on British locomotive works, and the first train bound for the east steamed out of Kalgoorlie on October 25, 1917.

Opposite: The train ferry 'Lake Baikal' (top left) used to carry trains across the lake, before the railway opened. The more ambitious trains of the Wagons-Lits company (centre) ran from St Petersburg (now Leningrad) to Vienna and then across northern Italy to Nice on the French Riviera. Below left: General Kuropatkin, commander of Russian forces during the Russo-Japanese war lunching with his staff in his luxurious dining car.
The railway across the desert Nullarbor plain in central Australia is the longest stretch of straight line in the world (328 miles); a track laying machine (above) and a string of camels (below) used in the transcontinental construction project.

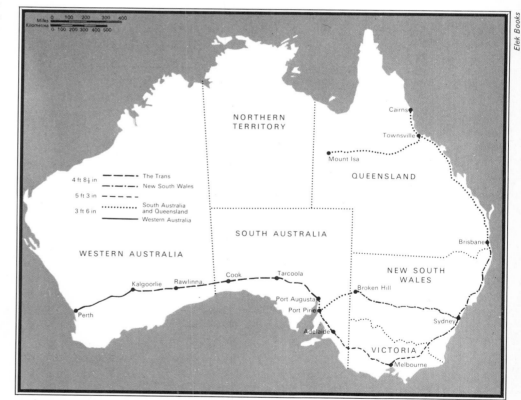

Elek Books

J. L. Buckland

Illustrated London News

Mary Evans

In Africa, the great railway visionary was Cecil Rhodes. "The railway is my right hand, the telegraph my voice," he said on one occasion, and he dreamed of a railway running all the way from the Cape of Good Hope to Cairo.

But it was greed for wealth that had prompted the building of the first railways north from the Cape – to Kimberley after the discovery of diamonds in 1869, to the Transvaal after the discovery of gold in 1886 – and the riches locked up in the soil of Africa, rather than imperial vision, continued to dictate to a large extent where railways were built, except in the case of Rhodes, already wealthy and powerful enough to indulge his dream.

In 1887 he won Rhodesia – larger than Spain, France and Germany put together – for the British Empire and soon began work on what he believed was the first stage of the Cape-to-Cairo railway.

Bulawayo, in the south of Rhodesia, was reached in 1897, and the line pushed on north-eastward, through untamed bush, to the Zambezi river and the mighty Victoria Falls. It was an epic piece of railway construction with the workers facing the constant threat of being struck down by tropical diseases or eaten by lions.

Lions on the line

The English contractor George Pauling has described one encounter with a pride of lions, resting in a side cutting as the construction train chugged towards them at a mere four mph: "It was an awe-inspiring sight, and the driver was for a moment nonplussed. He knew that he dare not increase speed and run the risk of derailment.

"There was not a gun on the train. Few men are valiant in the immediate presence of wild lions, and we three 'passengers' deemed it expedient to scramble out of the truck and on to the side of the engine away from the herd.

"With a view to making as much noise as possible the driver opened his whistle and cylinder cocks and commenced to creep past the place where the lions were resting. The noise was too much for them, for they all bolted with the exception of one stately old lioness, who stood her ground and snarled at us as we passed.

"Had we remained in the truck it is not improbable that she would have made a jump at one of us, but she funked the engine and its steam and noise . . ."

Except for North America, where the Mallet articulated locomotive was used exclusively, the best-known articulated type was the Garratt. H. W. Garratt designed his first articulated locomotive in 1909 and they have been used all over the world, particularly in southern Africa. This one was built in 1915 for the 5ft 3in gauge Sao Paulo Railway in Brazil.

Mary Evans

Royal Commonwealth Society

Mansell

The Bechuanaland Railway ran northwards from Vryburg in South Africa to Bulawayo. Far left: The scene at Bulawayo on the arrival of the first train in 1897 and fording a river at Bulawayo. Building the Transvaal railway (above left) in the early 1890s and the first railway bridge across the Vaal river being tested (left). Above: George Pauling, the South African engineer and contractor who secured the contract to build the first line in the Transvaal.

Stanley Livingstone was the first white man to see the spectacular Victoria Falls in 1855 and his description had captured the imagination of Rhodes to such an extent that he gave orders for the Zambezi to be spanned by a bridge built close enough to the Falls for their spray to wet each passing train.

The result was a spectacular piece of engineering with a cable-way, capable of carrying a load of ten tons, being built across the steep gorge so that the bridge could be built from both sides simultaneously. It was finally completed in April 1905.

But Rhodes, who had never seen the Falls, which are 1616 miles from Cape Town, never saw the bridge either. He had died three years earlier. His tomb is at Bulawayo where all trains today stop long enough for passengers to descend and pay their respects to the memory of the man who opened up the route on which they are travelling.

Rhodes left behind not only a railway line but a tradition of comfortable travel. The *Zambezi Express de Luxe*, which he introduced between Bulawayo and Cape Town in the year of his death, had 12 bogie coaches lit by electricity and featuring crimson leather upholstery and wine coolers.

One coach was a buffet car whose appointments included a library and reading room, a writing room, a card room, a smoking room and an observation balcony — a considerable design achievement for one coach on a narrow-gauge railway.

A civilizing influence?

Rhodes's dream of a through route from the Cape to Cairo was not realized, however. His line eventually reached Kindu in the Congo (now Zaïre). From there a gap of a thousand miles still exists before the lines of the Sudan are reached and there is a further gap of 150 miles between the Sudan railways and those of the Egyptian system.

In the Congo, conditions proved even worse than they had in Rhodesia. Stanley, newspaperman and explorer, had advised King Leopold II of the Belgians: "Without a railway, Your Majesty, the Congo is not worth a penny." The task of building a line to open up the interior occupied a large part of the 1890s.

The work was begun with a force of European artisans and tracklayers, backed by two thousand African labourers. The depredations of fever were appalling, mortality at one point reaching eight per cent. "Set us free," the Africans begged each morning before being cajoled into carrying on.

Curve followed curve, bridge followed bridge. Nobody bothered about workers who had the misfortune to fall into a river: the crocodiles would reach them before the rescuers. When the Africans finally went on strike, 500 Chinese, who had proved their toughness in building railroads in the United States, were imported. Within a few weeks more than half were dead or had deserted.

But, despite all the difficulties and the high cost in human life, a gaily-decorated locomotive steamed into Stanley Pool on March 16, 1898, 20 years to the day since the first white man had set foot there. The inaugural speech said: "The railway has put an end to those degrading caravans of people carrying loads on their heads single file through the jungle, taking 20 days for as many miles.

"It will transport vast treasures – hardwood, rubber, coffee and sugar cane – and in return bring to 30 million half-wild creatures the blessings of civilization . . ."

This is the spirit which animated the building of railroads north and south of the torrid Equator at this time: the white man would become richer and the black man, as something of an after-thought, would enjoy – or, at least, have a glimpse of – the blessings of the white man's civilization.

In opening up the Dark Continent, however, the railways also began the accelerating process of opening the eyes and minds of Africans, with dramatic political consequences in our own time.

Above left: Laying the rails between Kindu and Kongolo in Zaïre in the early 1900s. Right: Time table and map of the Cape to Cairo Railway showing the sections that were never completed. Opposite, top: Building the Victoria Falls bridge across the gorge of the Zambezi river in 1905. Centre: A Coach interior on the Zambezi Express, which carried tourists to the Victoria Falls in Rhodesia early in the twentieth century (left), and building the first railway in Zaïre from Matadi to Kinshasa in 1898.

Right: This little tank locomotive was built for the 2ft 6in gauge Kelani Valley railway in 1909. The line belonged to the Ceylon Government Railway and runs south-east from Colombo.

e Present
Route.

...ays.

...(via Belgian Congo)
7,074 miles.

... STATE RAILWAYS.

- - - - - 130 miles.
- - 149 miles. (1 Day).
...otian train) - - 555 miles. (1½ Days).
...Philæ-Assouan (Steamer), 208 miles (2 Days).

...VERNMENT RAILWAYS
...ND STEAMERS.

...Sudan train) - - 579 miles. 1½ Days.
...rtoum (train) - - 240 miles. (1 Day).
...n steamer) - - 890 miles. (14 Days).

...A MARINE STEAMERS.

...oro-Rejaf (Uganda Marine Steamer) 273 miles.
...ahagi (Lake Albert), (motor road), 683 miles.
...(8 Days).
...tanleyville (train) - - - 77 miles.
...rville (steamer) - - - 196 miles.
...a (rail) - - - - 217 miles.
...eyville - - - - (10 Days).

... RAILWAYS AND STEAMERS.

...gola (steamer) - - - 398 miles.
...m Cape Town (by rail), completed 1918, 2,632 miles.
...(Travelled in 6 Days by train).

...ANGA JUNCTION RAILWAYS.

...MA and KATANGA - - - 666 miles.
...to Elizabethville (train) - - 655 miles.
...Broken Hill - - - - (3 Days).
...Elizabethville

...RHODESIAN RAILWAYS.

...Bulawayo (train) - - - 490 miles.
...Mafeking (train) - - - 123 miles.
...o Kimberley (train) - - 647 miles.
...to Bulawayo - - - - (3 Days).

... AFRICAN RAILWAYS AND PORTS.

...Cape Town (by Union Castle Line) - 6,201 miles.
...(18 Days).

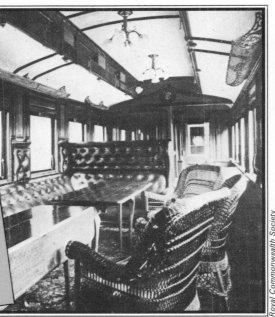

THE LOCOMOTIVE CAB

The cab of express locomotive No. 1 of the Great Northern Railway in England, built 1870. By this date the main controls had settled down into the form that lasted until the end of steam locomotive building. Extra apparatus was later added to this basic, bare form of cab.

1. Boiler steam pressure gauge. From 50lb per square inch in the early days, the pressure had crept up to 120lb per square inch by 1870 and was to reach 275lb per square inch by the end of the steam locomotive era.

2. Spectacle glass.

3. Regulator. This controls the amount of steam entering the cylinders.

4. Injector control for filling the boiler with water (one each side).

5. Blower cock. This directs a jet of steam up the chimney for drawing the fire when the locomotive is not moving.

6. Boiler water level gauge. For safety reasons two were provided in later years.

7. Reversing gear lever. This was not only used to reverse the valve gear, but also to control the quantity of steam entering the cylinder for each piston stroke.

8. Boiler washout plugs. Periodically the boiler is washed free of accumulated scale by water jets. These plugs in the cab allow the top of the firebox to be cleaned.

9. Cylinder cocks. Opened upon starting to allow any condensed water accumulated in the cylinders to be blown out by the steam.

10. Injector delivery pipe. This delivers fresh water into the boiler.

11. Dry sand. By opening the valve sand is delivered under the driving wheels to prevent slipping, particularly when starting.

12. Fire hole door, through which the fireman feeds the coal fuel.

13. Footplate on which members of the loco-motive crew stand.

14. Ashpan fire damper control. This regulates the air supply to the fire.

15. Rear carrying wheel springs.

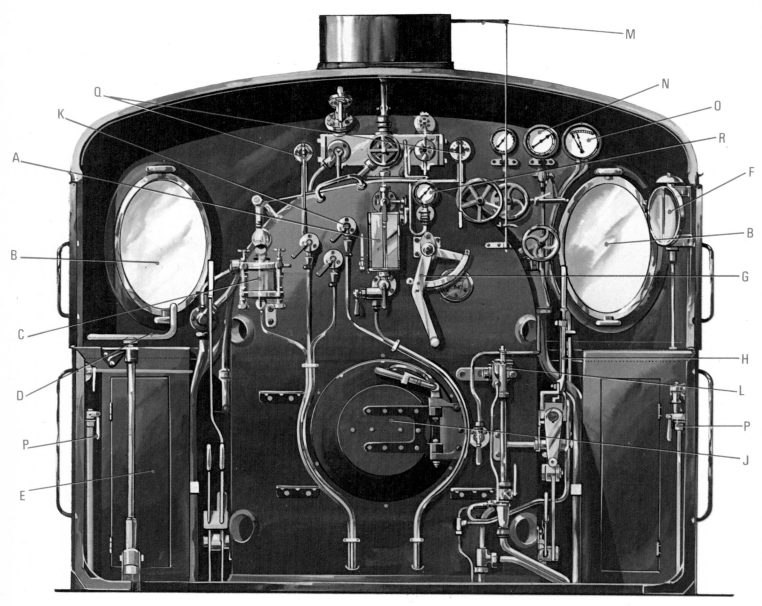

K · Q · O · M · N · O · R · A · F · B · B · G · C · H · L · D · P · E · P · J

Side view of a reversing lever

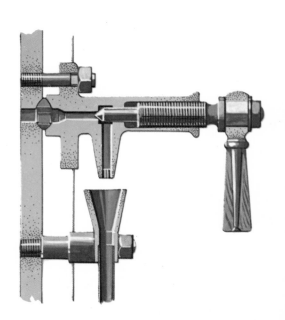

Section of a boiler water level test cock

THE LOCOMOTIVE CAB

The cab layout of a Hungarian State Railways' Class 375 two-cylinder compound tank locomotive designed in 1907

A. Boiler water level gauge

B. Glass spectacle — the whole front of the cab structure is known as the spectacle plate

C. Sight feed lubricator for the cylinders — when working the drops of oil may be seen passing through the glass

D. Hand brake control

E. Cupboard

F. Tachometer to indicate and record the speeds attained

G. Regulator to admit boiler steam to the cylinders

H. Reversing lever — a side view of which is shown below, on the left. The smaller handle is used to lock the reversing lever proper into any required position

J. Firehole door

K. Boiler water level test cocks — a section of a cock is shown bottom right

L. Air brake control valve

M. Whistle lever

N. Gauge showing steam pressure between high pressure and low pressure cylinders

O. Double pressure gauge for pressures in air brake system

P. Water supply valves (right- and left-hand) for the injector to impel water into the boiler

Q. Steam supply valves (right- and left-hand) for the injector to impel water into the boiler

R. Boiler steam pressure gauge

INDEX

Page numbers in roman type indicate a text reference; numbers in *italic type* indicate illustrations.